CINCINNATI
POWER
BASKETBALL

ED JUCKER

HEAD BASKETBALL COACH
UNIVERSITY OF CINCINNATI
NCAA CHAMPIONS 1961 AND 1962

CINCINNATI
POWER
BASKETBALL

1962

PRENTICE-HALL, INC.   Englewood Cliffs, N.J.

© 1962

PRENTICE-HALL, INC.

Englewood Cliffs, N.J.

LIBRARY OF CONGRESS
CATALOGUE CARD NO.: 63-7840

PRINTED IN THE UNITED STATES OF AMERICA
13369-C

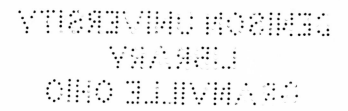

To my wife, Joanne, my assistant coaches, Tay Baker and John Powless, and to the players who earned these titles:

NCAA BASKETBALL NATIONAL CHAMPIONS 1962
NCAA BASKETBALL NATIONAL CHAMPIONS 1961
NCAA MIDWEST REGIONAL CHAMPIONS 1962
NCAA MIDWEST REGIONAL CHAMPIONS 1961
CO-CHAMPIONS, MISSOURI VALLEY CONFERENCE 1962
CHAMPIONS, MISSOURI VALLEY CONFERENCE 1961
CHAMPIONS, NEW YORK HOLIDAY TOURNAMENT 1961

ED JUCKER, BASKETBALL, and the UNIVER-
VERSITY of CINCINNATI are all bound together
in this great coaching book just as they are in the true-
life story of their glorious successes in the sport. This
book is more than a text, more than a treatise, more
than an offensive and defensive manual—it is the *life*
of a great coach, his philosophy, techniques, tactics,
strategy, and the "inside" secrets which have combined
to lift him and his type of basketball to the heights.

Nothing has been left out of this "Cinderella" story
of basketball success. In this book you will find the philosophy behind Ed Jucker's team play and his offensive and defensive systems (with more than 80 diagrams
and complete descriptions).

You might think that Ed Jucker's career started at
the top where he now stands as America's leading coach.
This is not true. I knew Ed when he was an outstanding college athlete at Cincinnati where he played base-
ball, basketball (captain in 1939-1940 and selected on
several All-Ohio teams), and was an outstanding golfer.
I remember Ed as a young college graduate who was
"possessed" with a burning desire to make his mark as
a basketball coach. The youngster "breathed" basketball.
He attended clinics, made voluminous notes, charted
games, and discussed basketball with anyone and everyone he thought could help him develop "his" style of
play.

Ed Jucker was different from most aspiring neophytes

FOREWORD

who dreamed about coaching success. *He* did something about it! He didn't let his dreams and hopes die on the vine. He hustled at *his* game until he got a coaching job. And, once on his way, he didn't talk about bad breaks or losing seasons (if he had any). Years of dreaming, and planning and working went into the apprenticeship of this man. He kept his dream ever before him and he kept hustling, and when his big chance came—he was ready. Ed justified the confidence and judgment of the man whose assistant he was for seven years—George Smith, now Director of Athletics at Cincinnati.

Today, Ed Jucker is a poised, outspoken, confident coaching master of the game he loves. He believes in himself, his style of play, and in his players. Nothing, but nothing, is as important to Ed as basketball. He is patient as a coach and popular with his players, who respect him as their leader and admire him as a friend. His stirring victories and great successes have left him unchanged. He is a humble man.

Ed is a fiery competitor and fights to score and save every point. A stickler for detail, he is tactically perfect in his approach to meeting a strong competitor. And, like Adolph Rupp when it comes to evaluating his team's chances, Ed concedes nothing—to *any* opponent.

Ed believes in scouting, movies of past games, and strategy (his own special brand). His devotion to all the facets of coaching resulted in the 1961 under-dog upset which ended mighty Ohio State's thirty-two game winning streak and brought Cincinnati the National Championship. Then, just to prove this accomplishment was no flash in the pan, Ed and his gang took up in 1962 right where they had left off the year before and did it all over again!

During his tenure as head basketball coach at Cincinnati (two years), the "Bearcats" have won 56 games while losing but 5 against the best teams in the country. Ed's Bearcats have won the National Championship twice, the Midwestern Regionals twice, the tough Missouri Valley Conference twice, and the Holiday Festival in Madison Square Garden. Cincinnati has bested the toughest competition in the United States, beating the "Big Ten" Conference champs (Ohio State), the "Big Five" champs (U.C.L.A.), and the "Big Eight" champs (Colorado). The N.I.T. champion (Dayton) and runner-up (St. John's) also fell before their might.

Hop on Ed Jucker's band wagon and string along with the winner who built two National Championship teams in two consecutive years with a disciplined and deliberate pattern-offense and a hustling, leech-

FOREWORD

like defense. Ed's championship philosophy is built on "the *good* shot and *great* defense."

You will find all the details in this book—a sure-fire offense based on short, sharp passes designed to free the shooter for the close-in shot and a "hard-nose" switching defense coupled with a strong rebounding game. Ed's book contains all the information vital to the coaching of championship basketball. Don't miss it!

CLAIR BEE

A great many books have been written about basketball during the 22 years that I have been connected with the game. I am sure I have not read them all, but I have read enough of them to form the opinion that their authors are realistic men. A realistic man, you understand, is a basketball coach who is quite willing to instruct us in the generalities of the game, but is understandably wary of revealing his own trade secrets. Practical circumstances, such as won-lost records, dictate that a book by a coach-author contain information on the art of dribbling (don't look at the ball), the science of ankle wrapping (wrap the whole team, so your opponent won't know who's hurt), and the minimum hours of sleep required to keep a growing seven-foot boy growing.

It is neither realistic nor practical to outline the offense that you intend to use next March in the NCAA Tournament. Paragraphs describing Dr. Naismith's famous peach basket, on the other hand, are allowable. It is my own feeling, however, that readers are beginning to tire of the realistic, practical approach. The book you are about to read, therefore, is completely unrealistic.

It does not describe offenses and defenses that are either common information, or as out of date as the peach basket. It assumes that you have a knowledge of the fundamentals of the game. It contains an exact description of the system of basketball that won two Na-

PREFACE

PREFACE

tional Championships for the University of Cincinnati. What you will read about in this book, we use on the basketball floor. Every play we run, every defense maneuver we make, can be found here.

A large part of our basketball system is original, as it should be. Some is borrowed and refined. To explain the unique quality of our offensive attack I have included more than 80 diagrams straight from the files in my office. Full descriptions of all options and adjustments are included, as well as references to games in which certain aspects of our system were especially successful. If you are a spectator-reader, I trust that this exposition of the means a major basketball team used to win two successive NCAA Championships will add to your enjoyment of the game as a whole. If you are a coach-reader, I hope I can offer something useful to your own particular situation. If you are a player-reader, perhaps the Cincinnati story will prove an inspiration.

I suspect that there are many who will question the sincerity of a coach who proclaims that he is about to bare his innermost secrets to the public. To those, I add this note: Basketball is a great and dynamic sport, constantly improving. If one suggestion in this book will add to or benefit the game, I shall have achieved my object in writing it. I am confident that the ideas contained in these chapters will not remain static. Many coaches, including this one, will continue to modify and improve these ideas in the future.

In addition, I am convinced that, over the long haul of any season, the winning of basketball games will not depend upon what is published in books, but will depend, as always, upon the caliber and training of the boys who play the game.

ED JUCKER

ACKNOWLEDGMENTS

Many people have contributed indirectly to the story that is told in this book. Among them I should like to mention George Smith, Athletic Director of the University of Cincinnati, who gave me the opportunity to test my ideas as a head coach and lent encouragement every step of the way; team physician, Dr. Don Jacobs, and team trainer, Joe Keefe, who kept the boys in shape for the grueling power basketball described here; and Dr. William Schwarberg, Assistant Athletic Director and Faculty Representative, who handled the great mass of details that make up a major basketball traveling schedule.

In addition I wish to express my sincere thanks to the people who were directly concerned with the preparation of this book: Hod Blaney, University of Cincinnati Sports Publicity Director, for research and statistics; William R. Whitteker, Bearcat Photographer, Wideworld Photos, and Clockson for still pictures; Don Galvin, Team Photographer, for game and practice films; Alice Portune, for drawing the diagrams; and Dr. Peter Garvin, for inspiring the project.

My special thanks is extended to Robert Portune for his literary assistance in the organization and preparation of the text of this book.

ED JUCKER

CONTENTS

CONTENTS

CONTENTS

KEY TO DIAGRAMS

OFFENSE	DEFENSE
P Pivot Man	① On Pivot Man
F Strong Side Forward	② On Strong Side Forward
f Weak Side Forward	③ On Weak Side Forward
G Strong Side Guard	④ On Strong Side Guard
g Weak Side Guard	⑤ On Weak Side Guard

⟶ Path of player

- - -⟶ Path of ball

⋀⋀⟶ Dribble

Pick or screen

NOTE: In this book the designation *Strong Side* applies to the offensive overload in a play pattern.

CINCINNATI
POWER
BASKETBALL

On a June night in 1960 a tall young man stepped forward under the lights in the University of Cincinnati's Nippert Stadium and received his diploma. In that instant a basketball era ended.

During his collegiate varsity career Oscar Robertson, the fabulous "Big O," had accounted for 2973 points and 1338 rebounds. Three times he had led the Cincinnati Bearcats to the championship of that graveyard of basketball ambitions, the Missouri Valley Conference. Twice he had led them into the NCAA Semi-Finals. In three years of major collegiate competition the Bearcats, with All-American Robertson, had developed a run-shoot-run offense that swept opponent after opponent off the court, establishing a record of seventy-nine games won and nine games lost. In those three years rabid University of Cincinnati fans had never seen a Bearcat team lose at home.

Graduating with Robertson that fateful June night were an outstanding guard named Ralph Davis, who boasted 1103 points in his varsity career, and Larry Willey, holder of the Missouri Valley Conference record for field-goal percentage.

After Oscar Robertson, What?

As newly appointed head coach of the University of Cincinnati basketball team, I viewed the 1960 Commencement Exercises with a variety of emotions, none

THE CINCINNATI STORY

of them joyous. Just in case I had forgotten, the local newspapers reminded me that (a) I had lost 55 of our 87 point per game average, (b) I had lost an average of 21 rebounds per game, (c) tickets were sold out for the 1960-61 home season, and (d) there was a long line of fearsome opponents waiting to get revenge for defeats suffered over the three years just past.

In answer to a question, I said, "There is not going to be any drop in the quality of University of Cincinnati basketball; this year's team will rank among the nation's leaders." The UPI, which had rated Cincinnati no lower than third in our two previous seasons, promptly ranked us nineteenth. The kindest prediction delivered before the season opened was that we might, with luck, "finish second in the MVC."

Thirty games later the University of Cincinnati was crowned National Champion after defeating Ohio State University in the NCAA Finals at Kansas City. Exactly one year later, in March of 1962, the University of Cincinnati Bearcats became the fourth team in the history of the NCAA Tournament to win two consecutive championships, once more defeating Ohio State in the Finals.

How did it happen? The answer is not, as some have stated, a Cinderella story. Cinderella, you will recall, had a fairy godmother going for her through the whole game. The University of Cincinnati basketball squads, on the other hand, had no magic but teamwork—the kind of teamwork and determination and desire that enabled the players on these squads to learn a whole new system of play before the 1960-61 season began and to develop it so well during less than one month of competition that they were able to fight their way from a five won, three lost record in December of 1960 to a string of 22 straight victories over the remainder of the season. Using the same system in 1961-62, that season's team won 29 games and lost 2, and emerged as the Number One team in the nation.

I intend to disclose every detail of this successful system in the chapters that follow.

To understand the philosophy underlying our type of play, it is necessary that you understand the type of players who perfected it. Individually, we have had no "super-stars." Collectivelly, we have had what I have been proud to call, "All-American *teams.*" In the beginning we had the kind of talent available to most coaches—a nucleus of good, solid veterans and some promising sophomores. Some height, some speed, and some good shooters. No more and no less.

"There are two ways of achieving recognition," I remember telling the team in one of our early meetings. "One way is to have a star player who can lead you in a wide open, fast-breaking, spectacular game that will have the crowd screaming for you even when you lose. The other way is to win." Because the loss of the incomparable Robertson eliminated any consideration of the first method, we were left with only one choice. *We had to win.*

Winning a basketball game has been described in absurdly simple terms as the process of scoring more points than your opponents. If a team lacks an exceptional shooter, the brunt of the scoring cannot fall upon one individual but must become a team effort. It has always been my theory that a system of offense that divides the scoring among all members of a team is a more potent system than one which sets up opportunities for a single shooter. Only once in a lifetime does an Oscar Robertson come along to shake that theory. I must remind those who never saw Robertson play, however, that he was not only the greatest shooter in college history, but also one of the greatest team players the game has known. His genius for playmaking, his record of seven assists per game, and his defensive ability are too often forgotten.

A New System of Play for Cincinnati

At the beginning of the 1960-61 season our need for team scoring was acute. Somehow we had to devise a system that would make up most of the 55 points per game that graduation had subtracted from our average. The heart of that system would have to be scoring opportunity for all five positions—that is, planned opportunity. In short, a pattern offense.

Abilities to score vary from man to man, of course. Some players are better at the jump shot than others, some are better at hook shots, some are better at set shots. *But all men are better close to the basket.* Close shots build confidence in even the poorer shooters. Close shots, to put it bluntly, equalize abilities. In our situation a close-in attack was an absolute necessity. Scoring opportunities had to be developed in the area nearest the basket. We planned the new Cincinnati offense, therefore, to bring the maximum scoring opportunity for all five men within a tight semi-circle whose radius was the distance from the foul line to the basket. In order to move men into this restricted area from any position and still not neglect defense against a turnover, we devised a disciplined pattern offense, supported by a man-to-man pressure defense, and set out to weld a team.

The burden of converting from a run-shoot-run offense to a more deliberate style of play fell upon the 1960-61 Cincinnati Bearcats. Old habits had to be broken, especially the understandable tendency to look for Robertson to make the big play when the situation on the floor became critical. In addition, there was the tendency, also understandable, on the part of each individual to try to step into the vacated role of superstar. Tom Thacker, our fine sophomore forward on that team, summed it up after the season when he said, "At the beginning of the year we were all trying to be All-Americans. After Seton Hall we settled down to become a team."

We lost three of our first eight games in 1960-61 to Seton Hall, St. Louis, and Bradley. The last two were Missouri Valley Conference games, and they marked the first time we had ever lost two consecutive games in the conference. Then, on December 29, with 1960 fast running out, and trailing the University of Dayton by eleven points, the entire system of pattern offense and pressure defense blended into a distinct style. We won by 10 points that night, and 21 games later we were National Champions.

The final game of the 1961 NCAA Tournament offers proof, if proof is needed, of the manner in which that year's Cincinnati team perfected the new system. On offense, four of the five starters scored in double figures. On defense, they held one of the greatest scoring teams in collegiate history to only 50 shots from the field. As a clincher, our players turned the ball over *just three times*.

The following year, using the same system, we recovered from two early season conference losses (by a total of three points) and went on to a season's record of 29 and 2, winning our last 18 straight games. A measure of our players' mastery of our system of pressure defense is the fact that in the conference playoff game against Bradley, and in our two successive NCAA Regional Tournament games, we held each opposing team to 46 points per game.

Before the 1960-61 season, University of Cincinnati followers were concerned when I announced that my first act as head coach would be to change our style of play from run-shoot-run to a pattern offense. I assured them then, and I am just as emphatic now, that a deliberate style of play, using high-percentage shots from close to the basket should not be confused with slowdown, hold-the-score-down, drive-the-crowd-away basketball. Spectators deserve more than that. It is one thing to work for a good shot; it is another to hold the ball and pass up shots merely to play a low-score ball game.

My idea of pattern offense has its emphasis on the attack. Slow-down, ball control systems, on the other hand, use the offense as a defensive measure. Games in which one team refuses to shoot are not games at all; they are exercises in frustration. They kill interest among spectators and players alike. I am not referring to a last-minute freeze, however. A freeze in the final moments of a close game is a dramatic and thoroughly scientific maneuver. But a 40-minute stall is not my idea of basketball.

My "All-American Teams"

The two championship teams that I have called "All-American" were great in every single aspect of the game because the individual players were good in all departments. I think it is important that I describe the talents of these boys, at least briefly, to give you some understanding of the personnel we had in mind when we devised the system that is described throughout this book.

Our big center, Paul Hogue, looked awkward, but his size was deceptive. Actually he was very quick for a big man, and he possessed many fine moves at the pivot. At close range he was a deadly shot. Working inside the tight limits of our patterns, Hogue was almost impossible to handle. Many of our plays were designed with pivot screens because of his quick reactions and his strength. During his last two seasons he became one of the most respected centers in college basketball through sheer hard work and attention to detail.

Co-captain of the 1960-61 team was forward Bob Wiesenhahn, tagged "a monster" by his opponents. A rugged rebounder, Wiesenhahn was a bull of a man who used his tremendous strength to make up for his lack of height. Teamed with Hogue, he gave us great power under the boards. He, too, was a dangerous shooter in close. Above all, he had a burning desire to win, and his competitive spirit kept the team fired up throughout the season.

Tom Thacker, who played forward as a sophomore and learned to play guard as a junior, was "the tallest 6′ 2″ player in basketball." Thacker is blessed with natural ability and has the fastest hands I have ever seen. With these talents, it is only right that he should be utilized to his full ability. Because he is a natural free-lancer, his movements could have been inhibited by a pattern offense. In our system, however, the free-lancer is given better opportunities to use his individuality without constantly facing a one-on-one situation.

Guard Carl Bouldin, our other co-captain in 1960-61, was a poised, well-disciplined quarterback whose job it was to direct traffic and set the tempo of our attack. His coolness under pressure often resulted in a clutch basket. In the NCAA Finals in 1961 Bouldin calmly pumped in four consecutive long jump shots just as it appeared that Ohio State was going to start sagging his defensive man. A steady playmaker of Bouldin's caliber was a necessity in our style of attack.

Tony Yates, at guard on both championship teams, is the best defensive player in collegiate basketball. A dedicated expert in the art of pressuring his opponent, he is superbly trained in all fundamentals. In competition he plays a fierce man-to-man defense, always all-out, with a good-natured smile permanently etched on his face. I suspect that this is maddening to the opposition, but it is typical of a young man who loves the game. Our system fits him like a glove; much of it was designed for him.

Like our 1960-61 team, which had sophomores Thacker and Yates playing as regulars, our 1961-62 team also had two sophomores, both forwards. Ron Bonham is one of the best shooters in the college ranks. He is also strong and coachable. His great touch makes him tremendously valuable to our offense, and our offense gives him greater freedom to shoot without having to force his shots. With his fine attitude and his desire to learn every phase of the game as well as he can, he fits into our system without difficulty.

At the other forward on our second championship team we had George Wilson, an exceptional jumper with good speed. His ability to anticipate and block a shot is a great defensive asset, and he is a good shooter and rebounder. Like Bonham, he has grown fond of our system and has developed into an outstanding all-around ball player.

On our bench we have had strong reserves to take up the slack when necessary. Tom Sizer, at guard, had the ability to come into a ball game fully attuned to the tempo, situation, and action, as if he had been playing from the start. This is a gift, and I know of no way to teach it. But a coach should always be on the lookout for such a player.

Fred Dierking, a forward, was toughest under pressure. Dale Heidotting was a master of the techniques required by our system. Larry Shingleton, the smallest man on the squad, was a lightning-like ball handler and dribbler. Other players had advantages of size, agility, or skill that made them valuable in certain situations. And here is the key to bench strength and substitution. For the man who enters a ball game as a substitute comes on to do a specific job, and he must be a specialist in that job, in addition to being a good all-around player. A coach who does not anticipate the situations that call for substitution and, thus, fails to prepare his reserves for those situations puts his team at a disadvantage. Five men alone do not make a championship team.

Each of the players I have described had to adapt himself to a system of play that was entirely new to him, and each had to learn the rigid discipline required to operate that system successfully. To these young men goes the credit for helping to return basketball to its original spirit of team play. The fact that these players were, for the most part, overlooked by the selectors of individual All-Americans somehow fades before their record of 56 victories and 5 defeats over a two-year span. The Cinderella story, which made interesting reading for a while, has also faded, and with it the theory that there was an element of luck in the success of the Cincinnati Bearcats. The team with discipline, desire, and pride in itself makes its own luck—without the help of a fairy godmother.

The Winning Tradition

Success is a combination of many ingredients. This is as true in basketball as it is in any other endeavor. For this reason no book about Cincinnati basketball would be complete without a reference to some of the ingredients that have led to the quality of the sport now being played here. Much of the credit for our present success belongs to assistant coaches Tay Baker and John Powless. Baker, one of the strictest fundamentalists in the game today, is an exceptional scout. Powless, our freshmen coach, is a keen student of the game and its players. The ability of these men to drill the reserves and freshmen in the systems of play used by our opponents is phenomenal. Scrimmages against these "red-shirt" teams have been a major factor in our performance. Needless to say, the "red shirts" and their mentors delight in beating the National Champion varsity regulars.

The part played by my predecessors, especially Cincinnati's present athletic director, George Smith, cannot be overemphasized in any discussion of Bearcat basketball traditions. In eight seasons as head basketball coach, "Genial" George won 154 games and lost 56. His teams won three consecutive Missouri Valley Championships, two NIT bids, a third place in the NCAA Midwest Regionals, and two third places in the NCAA Finals. And before George Smith, a Bearcat team under John Wiethe earned a bid to the NIT at Madison Square Garden in 1951.

The winning tradition at Cincinnati, as you can see, has become established over the past decade, as the center of basketball power has swung to the Midwest.

ILLUSTRATION I

National Champions, 1960-61. Front row, left to right: Calhoun, Yates, Bouldin, Hogue, Wiesenhahn, Thacker, Sizer. Back row, left to right: Ed Jucker (Head Coach), Shingleton, Dierking, Reis, Heidotting, Altenau, Tay Baker (Assistant Coach).

ILLUSTRATION II

National Champions, 1961-62. Front row, left to right: Shingleton, Yates, Elsasser, Thacker, Sizer, Calhoun. Back row, left to right: Tay Baker (Assistant Coach), Abernathy, Dierking, Wilson, Reis, Hogue, Heidotting, Bonham, Ed Jucker (Head Coach).

THE CINCINNATI STORY

A Coaching Philosophy

A coach's philosophy of the game he is coaching will be reflected in his attitude toward his players, in his respect for the spirit of the game, and in the systems of offense and defense that he adopts or adapts as his own.

Few aspects of basketball are brand new. Basketball fundamentals are as old as the hoop nailed to the garage door, and no newer than the one-handed jump shot. Fundamentals are the heart of the game, and the junior high or high school coach who neglects them does his boys an injustice. Shooting can be learned, but it takes years of practice to become great at it. A boy cannot begin learning to shoot in college. Nor can he begin learning to dribble there—or begin learning to pass, or run. Before he gets to college, a boy can also be taught the correct attitude toward the game. He will reflect his coach's own attitude, so the coach must teach by example. Among other more technical aspects of the game, a coach should remember that

SPORTSMANSHIP IS NOT A SIGN OF WEAKNESS

The true champions observe the rules. Fouling to injure a player has no place in basketball. The elimination of fouls should be a goal of every coach. Against Ohio State in the 1962 NCAA Finals our players committed *only three fouls* in the second half. Despite the fact that the National Championship was at stake, and that State's great Jerry Lucas wore a heavy bandage on his leg, no Cincinnati player would have considered "getting" Lucas. A tainted victory is no victory at all, no matter what the stakes.

GAMES ARE WON ON THE PRACTICE FLOOR

Winning teams practice harder than losing teams. And they practice to improve, not to pass away a pleasant afternoon in the gym. Every practice session should be well-organized, and every drill should have a definite purpose directly related to your offense or defense. Players who are too weary to give a hundred per cent effort in practice should be allowed to rest on the bench the night of the game. The so-called "star player" who loafs through practice needs a new coach. Great players are the hardest workers. Oscar Robertson always practiced as if he were in the midst of a championship game with the score tied and four seconds to play. Jack Twyman, one of the best shooters in professional basketball, was always the last man to leave the practice floor when he played for the University of Cincinnati.

10

THE CINCINNATI STORY

Too many young coaches waste too many hours devising "razzle-dazzle" offenses and freak defenses instead of concentrating on the simple elements that lead to success. The fewer passes needed to bring the ball into a good position for a shot, the better. The less dribbling, the better. Our own Swing-and-Go pattern, described in detail in Chapter 6, was designed to put tremendous offensive strength close to the basket in the simplest way possible, by stationing two big men there. Every move from there on is plain, time-tested, fundamental basketball, and fundamental basketball is like a chess game. Both sides know what moves are possible by the opposing forces, but the side that is quickest to react will counter the moves of the opposition. A few simple rules, drilled into the players, make their responses automatic. "If your man switches," we tell our center, "you roll to the basket." Automatically, every time, in every phase of our offense, if his man switches, our center rolls to the basket. Throughout our entire system of offense and defense, we strive for this kind of simplicity of response to the fundamental moves of our opponents. Like all sports, basketball is best when it is elemental, clearly defined, and uncluttered by frills or fads.

In addition to these general observations on the game, I am sincerely interested in seeing basketball knowledge circulated freely from coach to coach, from school to school, and from region to region. At clinic after clinic I have observed newcomers to the coaching ranks searching avidly for information that will help them improve the play in their own schools, and at clinic after clinic I have tried to explain our system in detail. Yet each time I have done so, I have come away with the impression that there are two reactions to the lectures of a successful coach: first, "he's keeping his real system secret," and, second, "he didn't give us that one, easy, follow-the-directions-on-the-bottle, magic formula for winning."

Friends, there are no secrets in this day of game movies and expert scouts. That is the reason the chapters to follow hide nothing. There are no surprises in these pages for the coaches of the Missouri Valley Conference. But perhaps there is something of value for the high school or college coach who has never seen Cincinnati play, and something of interest for the spectator who has never been able to discover how a major basketball team develops its offense and defense. Most important of all, perhaps a boy will find in the Cincinnati story the knowledge that basketball is not the province of supermen, but is, instead, a game played by five players, *working together as a team*. This will be the boy I want playing for me.

The University of Cincinnati National Championship Teams in 1960-61 and 1961-62 played percentage basketball. By that I mean that our offense and defense were deliberately geared to the methods of play that have the greatest mathematical chance of succeeding. On offense a system of attack was developed that would give us the best shots possible from the high-percentage areas under and near the basket. On defense, conversely, we concentrated on forcing our opponents to shoot from low-percentage areas, to take poor shots, and to grab off a lower percentage of rebounds than we did. The entire Cincinnati system, both offense and defense, will be described in detail in later chapters. For now, let us examine the mathematics involved.

The Good Shot

While it is true that many players are excellent shooters from outside, our feeling is that any player can be a good shooter in the high-percentage area close to the basket. In *Diagram 1* the areas, and my assessment of the probability of success from these areas, are illustrated.

The highest percentage of baskets per shot taken will occur in the semi-circle drawn tangent to the sides of the foul lane. It is here that lay-ups are made, and it is here that a team playing percentage basketball tries to concentrate its power. Next in scoring opportunity is

2

THE SCIENCE OF PER-

CENTAGE BASKETBALL

the area, 15 feet in diameter, bounded by the foul line and the arcs drawn off the foul line (shown in *Diagram 1*). Within this area occur the short jump shots, both one- and two-handed, and the hook shoots.

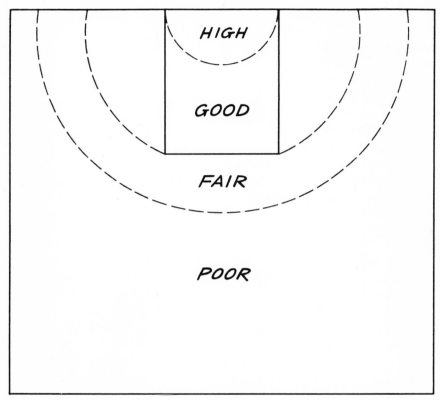

DIAGRAM 1

Probable success of shots in areas around the offensive basket.

Continuing out, like ripples from a stone dropped in a pool, the shooting areas diminish the chances of scoring in direct proportion to their distance from the basket. The semi-circle drawn from the top of the foul circle to the baseline is 21 feet from the basket, still a good area for a capable jump-shooter or set-shooter, provided he does not have to fight to get his shot off. Beyond this semi-circle, however, I consider the chances of scoring poor.

Our pattern offense was designed with these shooting areas in mind. And our defense is aimed at keeping the opposition out of the high-percentage areas. In addition, we know that a player who has to fight a one-on-one situation to get off a shot has less chance of scoring than a player who is free to shoot behind a screen, or a player whose defensive man has been picked. Consequently, each pattern of our offense is planned to give the potential scorer freedom to get off a shot without forcing it. At the same time, our defensive effort attempts to distort patterns and force shots. What we try to do on offense, we try to prevent on defense.

Perhaps the success of this twofold goal can best be illustrated by two shot charts of games we played in our second championship season. These charts show the spot on the court from which every shot is taken during a game. The numbers are the game numbers of the players, and a circled number indicates that the player scored a basket from the position shown. To illustrate defense, I have reproduced the shot chart of our opponent (Miami University). This chart shows Miami scoring during the first half. (See top of *Diagram 2*.) Our offensive effort can be seen clearly in the second chart (bottom of *Diagram 2*). Here, in the first half of our NCAA Tournament game against Creighton University, our power inside is clearly demonstrated.

Over the course of two championship seasons our Cincinnati teams, trained to take the good shot from our pattern offense, hit on 45 per cent of their attempts and averaged 73 points per game, while winning 56 games and losing 5. Analyzing our shot charts kept over those two seasons, I have found that our percentage from what I call the "poor shooting" area drops to about 30.

Individual Versus Team Performance

My stock answer, whenever I am asked how our team will fare against a particular star scorer, is, "One man will never beat us." This reply is neither a boast nor wishful thinking, but is, instead, a pure case of percentages. The mathematics of individual versus team performance is revealing, and it should be studied by every coach who contemplates the opponents he will face over a season.

During a two-year period, playing our system of pressure defense and disciplined pattern offense, we have limited our opposition to approximately 60 shots per game. For the sake of discussion let us assume that we are scheduled to meet a team on whose roster there is a super-star who shoots a fantastic 60 per cent, while averaging 24 points per game. In order to maintain his average, excluding foul shots, this player would

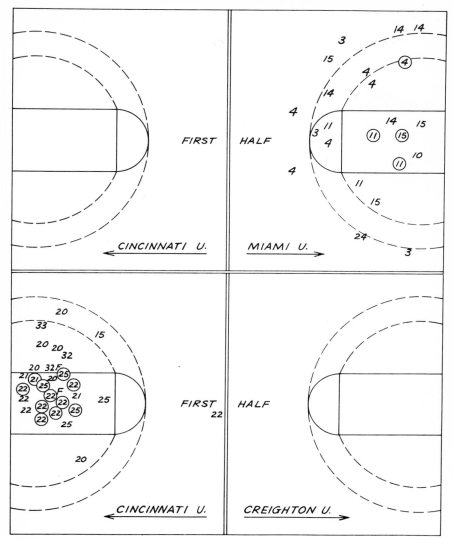

DIAGRAM 2

Shot charts showing Cincinnati system of defense and offense in action. Top shows shots taken by Miami University in game December 5, 1961. Bottom shows Cincinnati shots taken in NCAA Tournament game March 6, 1962.

have to take 20 shots. Statistically, this would leave 40 shots for the other four members of his team. Assuming that these men hit approximately 37 per cent of their shots (the average made against us over a two-year span), they would score 15 baskets, or 30 points among them. This would give our opponents 54 points on field goals. To top our two-year average score of 73 points per game, this team would have to add 20 points on foul shots, and 20 points is *exactly double the average scored against* us on free throws in the past. Such statistics, of course, do not win ball games, but they do help a coach determine a course of action. In our case, we play our normal defense, regardless of the reputation of any individual scorer.

Playing Percentages on Defense

Defensive strategy is concerned with preventing offensive scoring. The elimination of defensive fouls is part of percentage basketball, and we strive constantly to cut down on fouling, even though we teach a leech-like, pressure defense. During the 1961-62 season we were fifth in the nation in fewest personal fouls per game, *and fourth in the nation in defense!*

We consistently play percentages defensively by forcing our opponents to shoot from poor court positions, by making them take off-balance or forced shots, and by distorting the offensive patterns that our scouting reports reveal.

Against fast-breaking teams we have learned that the highest percentage of defensive success goes to the team that battles for the defensive rebound. Consequently, we will gamble a fourth man on the defensive boards when we face a fast-breaking opponent. Against Ohio State in the NCAA Tournament Finals in 1962, we gambled even more than that, as you will discover in the next chapter, and we stopped what was probably the greatest fast break in the country. Again, percentages were with us.

Statistics

Although we apply the science of percentages to our planning of offense and defense at the University of Cincinnati, we are not "statistic-happy." We can learn more about the performance of our players by studying movies than we can by analyzing their records. *Diagram 3* illustrates what I consider to be our most useful chart because it lists the factors I consider most important, as far as statistics are concerned. The last column, "Points Responsible For," represents the difference between a player's own personal scoring, and the scoring that resulted from his

U. of C. Record Chart

Date_____

OFFICIALS_____

U. of C. vs. _____ at _____

| Name | PF | Field Goals | | Foul Shots | | Loss of Ball | | | Possession | Rebounds | | Points |
		Made	Missed	Made	Missed	Pass.	Viol.	Fumb.	Gained	O	D	Responsible for

DIAGRAM 3

University of Cincinnati Record Chart, kept on each player.

fouls and turnovers. When this difference is negative, the player is hurting us rather than helping us, and improvement has to be made.

The scoring averages of individual opponents, while interesting, may not indicate much. It is more important, surely, to know what positions on the floor are high-percentage areas for each opponent, whether he is good with the right hand, the left hand, or both hands, what his favorite moves are, and how he reacts to certain defensive pressures. Given this information, we will try to defense him. Given his scoring average, we might feel that it is hardly worthwhile to show up for the game.

After a game the coaches may want to review the evening's statistics briefly, but during a game there are too many other problems to consider for a coach to burden his players with a résumé of the mathematics involved in their play. I sometimes glance at our first half shot chart as I go to the locker room between halves, but it cannot tell me anything I have not observed during the first 20 minutes of the game.

After the season, of course, it is pleasant to review all of the statistics that have been accumulated, if only to see how wisely you predicted what was going to happen. I predicted, for example, that our 1961-62 Bearcats could beat any team we could hold to 60 points or less. During that season we won 21 games in which my prediction came true. We won eight others, although our opponents scored more than 60 points in them.

I also predicted, as I indicated in chapter 1, that our style of basketball would succeed because it was team basketball, and end-of-season statistics have borne this prediction out. In the matter of team scoring, four of the five regulars on our 1960-61 National Championship squad averaged in double figures. In 1961-62 three of our starting five repeated this feat, and the fourth was only eight-tenths of a point away. Our combined offense and defense gave us per-game margins of victory in those two seasons of 14.2 and 17.1 respectively.

During those same two seasons the University finished with the longest winning streaks in major collegiate basketball, 22 straight games in 1960-61 and 18 straight in 1961-62. The Bearcats also closed out their home season by winning their seventy-seventh consecutive game in the city of Cincinnati.

These are some of the final statistics. If they indicate that the basketball system I am about to describe is designed to win games, then they have made their point.

What follows is the inside story of Cincinnati *power* basketball, as the Bearcats play it today.

In recent years the art of defense in all sports seems to have declined while coaches concentrated on the search for more baskets, more touchdowns, more home runs, and more points of all kinds in more ways than ever before. The increased emphasis on scoring may be attributed, in part, to a demand by spectators for bigger and bigger totals. This demand, supported by colorful tributes to the scorers in newspapers and magazines, has created an offense-minded, semi-hysterical cult of point worshipers across the nation. Some recent All-American basketball "teams" (I use the term loosely) have been composed of five centers, all high scorers, in a public example of the point-worshiping cult at its worst. All of this, I am convinced, tends to convert the game of basketball into an exhibition of basket shooting, dominated by individual heroes who are supported by a cast of unknown "feeders." Add to these developments the fact that defense is harder to teach and harder to learn than offense, and it becomes easy to understand why coaches and players neglect the defensive side of basketball.

One of the most difficult tasks undertaken by our coaching staff is that of convincing our young players that the secret of winning basketball games lies in defense. I would venture to say that this is the best kept secret in the land, so it comes as no surprise that players who are learning our system for the first time need to be sold on the idea. Much of our early season practice

3

INDIVIDUAL

PRESSURE DEFENSE

time, therefore, is devoted to selling defense to the individuals who are going to make up the team. A player who understands the importance of his own individual defensive play becomes a *whole* basketball player. Less than that is not enough, if the game is to remain a true team game.

The Defensive Attitude

Anyone capable of walking on a basketball court can play good defense. A large number of boys can play outstanding defense. A smaller, but still overwhelming, percentage of basketball players are capable of playing *great* defense, if only they can be brought to the proper mental attitude. The necessary ingredients that make up this attitude are PRIDE and DISCIPLINE.

To be an effective defensive man an individual must take pride in his work. He must be convinced that his ability to contain his man, to pressure him into making mistakes, and to harass him to the point of desperation throughout a ball game contributes mightily to the entire team effort. Unfortunately, the obstacles to be overcome before a coach instills such pride in his players are many. Great individual defense is largely overlooked or ignored in the headlines. Spectators fail to appreciate the skill—even the drama—of outstanding defensive play. Mere emphasis on defense during practice sessions will not instill pride. Such pride is only born of constant attention to the defensive play of each individual in games as well as practice. Coaches and team must be fully aware of individual defensive efforts, and the player responsible for defeating an offensive move should receive the plaudits of his coach and fellow team members. In addition, every player will play better defense if he is included in your scoring patterns. The guard who is only a feeder is hampered psychologically by the knowledge that his best efforts on defense will never lead to a scoring opportunity for him personally.

Cincinnati's Tony Yates, captain of the 1962-63 team, takes a fierce pride in his defensive ability. I have often called him the greatest defensive player in collegiate basketball, and for a reason. Yates knows the basic fundamental of defense, namely, that every blocked shot, every bad pass by an opponent, every missed basket, every turnover, and every disrupted offensive pattern is important to the outcome of the game. His consummate skill as a defensive guard stems from his knowledge that points lost are just as vital as points scored, when the final buzzer sounds. The object of the game, remember, is to score whenever you have the ball in your possession. A failure to score is a loss of points.

INDIVIDUAL PRESSURE DEFENSE

According to knowledgeable observers, the turning point of the 1962 NCAA Championship game came on a defensive play by Yates. As Ohio State's guards were bringing the ball into play after a Cincinnati basket, Yates suddenly darted between them, tapped the ball into the hands of teammate Tom Thacker, and had the satisfaction of seeing Thacker stuff the ball through the hoop; all of this within ten feet of the baseline! On that single effort Ohio State lost four points, its own two and Thacker's two.

The discipline required of each individual who plays effective defense is another factor that comes from knowledge of the contribution of defense to a winning season. Good discipline is that mysterious element the sportswriters call poise. In essence, it is the ability to do the job the way you learned the job, no matter what the stress or pressures of the game. A disciplined defensive man never takes the easy way out of a situation. He fights for position, he keeps his eyes on his man, he never relaxes pressure, and—most important—he follows the plan of defense developed for a particular game. Our two young sophomores, Ron Bonham and George Wilson, who contributed so much to our second National Championship Team in 1962, undoubtedly sacrificed some personal glory in disciplining themselves to our system, yet both realized the importance of their defensive assignments in each winning effort.

A prime example of such discipline was displayed by Bonham during the final game. Bonham, as everyone knows, is an exceptional shooter, one of the finest in the collegiate game. Against Ohio State, however, we assigned him an unenviable task. In the championship game we gave him the job of playing defense while on offense. That is, when we had the ball, Bonham's responsibility was to stay far outside in order to keep his defensive man, the great John Havlicek, away from the basket. With Havlicek removed from the defensive boards, Ohio State's fast-break potential was curtailed by about 50 per cent. In short, we used Bonham to help stop our opponent's most potent offensive weapon *while we still had the ball*. A less disciplined player would have found the assignment difficult to follow. Bonham, however, played the game we had planned. In that game he scored only three field goals—but Ohio State, with its fast break stalled, scored only 59 points instead of their average of 84!

Harassment, the Art of Forcing Mistakes

Our system of pressure defense is designed to force our opponents to distort their offensive patterns. Each individual on the Cincinnati team has the responsibility of harassing his man into mistakes. From the first day of practice we begin selling the idea of defense to our players, using a full-court press. While we seldom resort to a full-court press during the season, we have found that early practice of this kind teaches our players the elements of pressure defense that we want them to possess. Practicing man-to-man press drills teaches a player to think quickly, accustoms him to the tremendous physical effort needed to keep pressure on an opponent throughout a game, makes him hustle at all times on defense, and develops the knack of playing a man without losing sight of the ball. As an added value, such practice enables us to utilize the full-court press immediately on those rare occasions when we need it. Against Drake University, for example, early in the 1961-62 season we were trailing by nine points with only four minutes to play. Applying the press, we trapped our opponents enough times to close the gap and then go on to win by one point. Observers were surprised by our ability to steal the ball. What they did not realize was that we had been practicing trapping (double-teaming) constantly since the first day of pre-season drills.

Actually, our emphasis on the full-court press in practice has a double purpose. Not only do our players learn defense, but they also gain experience in bringing the ball upcourt against a press. On this point let me add that I have an axiom of practice that goes like this: "If you can't bring a ball across the center line against a one-on-one press, you can't play ball for us." Pitting our players against each other in such practice drills, therefore, gives our offense an opportunity to face some of the greatest defensive talent in the country. Our success against all kinds of presses during the past several seasons is proof that these drills pay off offensively as well as defensively.

Generally speaking, the pressure defense we expect of each individual on the Cincinnati team is not employed with the purpose of stealing the ball. Our defense, like our offense, is based on percentages, and percentagewise, the team that is forced to throw high or bad passes, take hurried or off-balance shots, or distort its usual attack is a team that suffers in the scoring column. Inevitably, a team that faces constant pressure will make mistakes. If these mistakes occur while the ball is being handled outside, we will trap (double-team) with a vengeance. Such trapping, however, is only one facet of pressure defense; it is not the sole objective.

ILLUSTRATION III

Maximum effort is required for pressure defense. Cincinnati's Bob Wiesenhahn shows the desire and determination that make defense "eighty per-
cent of the game."

The Defensive Guard

The defensive guard in our system is taught to vary the places at
which he starts to pressure his man. As his opponent comes up from the
end line, our guard may pick him up immediately, may pick him up
halfway to the center line, may pick him up at the center line itself, or
may even drop back into his own front court before harassing. The idea
is to keep the offensive man off balance mentally, so that he never is
quite sure when the pressure will start.

The guard on the man with the ball attempts to force him to the sideline so that he has only one direction to move. Once the ball moves into the front court, however, this guard overplays toward the side to which the most effective feed pass may come. For example, if the scouting report reveals that this feed is to a forward, the man with the ball is overplayed to the outside.

The guard on the man without the ball must be alert for a trap situation. If the offensive guards make the mistake of crossing, or if the man with the ball is tied up at the sideline, the guard on the man without the ball must be prepared to assist with the trap. Under all circumstances it is his responsibility to make it as difficult as possible for the ball to be fed to his man. He cannot overplay so much, however, that his man has an opportunity to cut behind him and go. Lunging is a defensive mistake that should be eliminated in practice sessions.

Defensive guards should keep in mind that the five-second count comes into effect if the guarded man with the ball cannot pass.

Once the ball is brought across the center line, our guards assume a well-balanced, parallel stance and use a slide step to move from side to side. Each is alert to a cut-behind by the other's man, and each must be prepared to pick up the other's man if such a cut-behind occurs. (Switching will be discussed in chapter 4.)

If the man with the ball is a good outside shooter, he must be played tight and jockeyed out of the floor position from which he scores best. At all times the offensive men must be pressured out of their usual patterns of attack. Successful individual defensive guard play results in bad passes, hurried shots, interceptions, traps, and time-outs, all of which contribute to the final result of any game.

The Defensive Forward

Of primary importance to the defensive forward is knowledge of the man he is guarding. Against a driver the defensive forward plays normal or loose; against a shooter he plays tight. In all cases the defensive forward has the responsibility of guarding the baseline. We teach our forwards to open up the baseline foot instead of standing parallel. This enables them to slide quickly and pinch their men to the endline, even if they have been faked. Sometimes, when a particular man is exceptionally adept at faking the defensive forward out of position, we find it necessary to overplay slightly toward the baseline. The object, always, is to force the offensive man to go high and wide instead of "going baseline."

INDIVIDUAL PRESSURE DEFENSE

In the event of a trap by the guards the defensive forward must be prepared to execute one of two necessary switches. If the free man is on his side, the defensive forward comes out and picks him up. If the free man is on the opposite side, the defensive forward plays in front of his man, and the defensive center zones.

The defensive forward, in normal play, drops off his man when the ball is on the other side. If he sees that the offensive center is overplaying the ball side, the defensive forward sags on him to guard against a drive or lob pass.

The defensive forward must always maintain good position on his man, remembering the three responsibilities listed below.

1. Prevent a pass in to your man.
2. If the pass is successful, force your man high and wide and disrupt his strongest offensive effort.
3. Whenever a shot is taken, box your man out and fight for the rebound.

Since most offensive attacks will include a forward pick, we have one cardinal rule to take care of such a situation. Our forwards are told, "If you are picked, go straight for the basket. Don't try to find your man until you are under the basket." The purpose of the pick is to free an offensive man for a drive to the basket, so we try to have someone there to greet him when he arrives. When this defensive reaction to the forward pick becomes automatic, the effectiveness of the pick is destroyed. The object of defense, remember, is to destroy the offensive attack, not just slow it down.

The Defensive Center

The defensive play of the center can be summed up in one sentence:

LET YOUR OPPONENT KNOW YOU ARE BOSS

Competition at the pivot spot is a test of strength, aggressiveness, and determination. A defensive center gains position through strength, and on defense position is all-important. There is no magic formula for establishing good defensive position against a capable pivot man, but two rules will help you find that position.

1. If the offensive pivot man is stationary, you must be in position to cut off his best game.
2. If the offensive pivot is moving to receive the ball, you must force him high and wide.

INDIVIDUAL PRESSURE DEFENSE

We instruct our centers in the primary responsibilities they must accept if they are to defend the danger zone near the basket. On most basketball teams today the offensive pivot man is the major scoring threat. All the outside defensive efforts by guards and forwards will be to no avail, therefore, if there is weakness in the middle. Our centers are told that they are responsible for preventing passes in to the pivot man, either by batting the ball away or by occasionally circling him. If he does receive the ball, the defensive center must be prepared to prevent a lay-up or a hook shot. Shots should be blocked on the upward flight of the ball, if fouls are to be avoided. A hand in front of the shooter's eyes helps make his shot more difficult. We call this "making him shoot through a picket fence."

We do not want our defensive center to switch on "give-and-go" situations up the middle. Instead, when the pivot man is used as a pick, our centers will fake the switch and reach out to delay the go-man until his defensive man can get him. Too many inexperienced boys fail to realize how effective this reaching can be in distorting an offensive pattern. It is one of the often-neglected details that makes the difference between a good defense and a so-so defense down the middle. The fact that the typical collegiate center has an arm span of almost seven feet should never be forgotten—but it is.

Knowing Your Opponent

The key to successful individual defense, as I have noted, is knowledge of the particular offense you are facing. A thorough scouting report is essential, and it is important that this report be prepared by a scout who is intimately acquainted with your own system and players. At Cincinnati this job is done by the coaches. Assigning scouting to a well-intentioned booster or alumnus may be good public relations, but it is a poor way to coach basketball. An effective scout does more than observe the strengths and weaknesses of your opponent; he also assesses these factors in the light of your own strengths and weaknesses. He must know your system and your players as only a coach can know them.

We have always provided our players with full descriptions of their individual opponents. In practice our "red shirt" team runs our current opponent's offense against our starting team, and the "red shirts" delight in making that offense work. Over and over again, first at a walk and then at full speed, our starters are forced to defend against the patterns they will be facing at game time, and over and over again we point out

26

the pressures and harassing that will disrupt these patterns. Each individual becomes aware of his own part in disrupting a particular offensive pattern. Decoy a man out of position, and this play cannot unfold. Force a pass here, or stop a dribble there, and this key play is disorganized. Keep Havlicek away from the defensive board, for example, and State's fast break will lose its effectiveness. Knowledge is power. The application of knowledge is the secret of good defense, as the following example indicates.

The place is Louisville, Kentucky, in March of 1962, nd we are one game away from our second National Championship. The previous evening we have watched Ohio State crush Wake Forest to gain the finals. In our practice session the day of the championship game we are analyzing the State offense. Bonham knows he is to keep Havlicek outside, but there are doubts. Suppose Havlicek is switched to another man. Suppose they see through our plan. "They won't take him off Bonham," we decide. All year Havlicek has guarded the best shooter; he is as proud of his defensive ability as our men are of theirs. "He will think he is holding Bonham down," we decide. "State will think they are defending Bonham like he has never been defended." Knowledge of our opponent makes us adopt the plan.

And what about Lucas? "Did you see what he did against Wake Forest? Here's the pattern." Noel, at guard, passes to Havlicek. Havlicek feeds Lucas, and Lucas rolls to the basket. Tough. But there's a chance of disrupting the pattern. Noel usually clears into the opposite corner after he passes. The Wake Forest man on him always followed him all the way. But Noel isn't dangerous in that corner. Okay, that's the answer. Thacker won't stay with him all the way, but will stop here on the foul lane. When Lucas receives the ball and rolls for the basket, surprise! Here's Thacker waiting to meet him. Ordinarily, a guard would have an impossible job trying to stop Lucas, but Thacker is a converted forward, with tremendous jumping ability. It is up to Paul Hogue, our great center, to force Lucas to go the way we want him to go. "Okay," Hogue says. With Hogue and Thacker working as planned, the play around the middle goes as planned. The pattern unfolds just as the "red shirts" ran it in practice, and we stop it.

Defense is a six man job. Five play; the other scouts.

Forearmed with a knowledge of his opponent, possessing skill in applying pressure, and filled with pride in his ability, a player will discover that playing defense can be a very satisfying experience. Too often coaches picture defense in mechanical terms, emphasizing the height of the hands, the position of the feet, and the angle of the upper torso. I would rather view man-to-man defense as essentially a single combat between well-trained and superbly conditioned athletes, one intent on getting the ball into a good position for a shot, the other intent on preventing that situation from developing. Offense is a matter of timed patterns. Upset the timing or change the pattern and the odds against its success mount. Individual pressure defense, with its harassing tactics, is designed to put unrelenting, aggressive force against the offense from the moment the ball is put into play.

Position and Moves

Position on the floor in relationship to your man is all-important in individual defense. Rule number one, of course, is not to allow your opponent to get between you and the basket. Secondly, it is best to overplay slightly toward the ball side, in order to intercept or bat away passes intended for your man. Movements should be made with a slide step, never by crossing the feet. In general, guards try to force their men away from the offensive strength, while forwards try to force their men away from the baseline. Good outside shooters are played tight and pressured into forced or off-balance shots.

The knowledge of whether your man has or has not used his dribble is vital. It is amazing how many defensive men cannot remember this one essential detail during the heat of play. It is also amazing how many players fail to talk on defense. Each individual must learn that the voice is a defensive tool, that it is used to alert teammates to impending picks or screens. Using your voice not only warns your teammates about situations developing out of their field of vision, but it also lets them know where you are. Good team defense requires each player to have a picture of the general pattern developing on the floor. His ears as well as his eyes must be used to form this picture.

Anticipating the Offense

In the combat between one offensive and one defensive player, the offensive man has a distinct advantage. He alone knows what his next move is going to be. The defensive man must anticipate that move in the light of what he knows of his opponent and his opponent's patterns of offense. The offensive player, he can be sure, will try to feint him out of position or fake him into committing himself. It is important, then, for the defensive player to retain good balance in order to make a move in any direction. Players should be adept at moving from side to side and to the rear with easy, controlled movements. These skills do not come naturally, but must be a part of every practice session. The Drills I have included in chapter 9 will show how we develop these skills in our own practice session. In practice, also, players should gain experience against head and shoulder fakes, eye feints, and bluffed throws. Players who leave their feet to block a bluffed throw or shot are caught in the most helpless defensive position possible. Unable to fly, a human being is out of his natural environment in the air. As a result, he is completely at the mercy of his opponent until he returns to the floor. The offensive man has little difficulty in forcing a foul by a jumping defender. The blocked shot or pass is a beautiful sight, but the foul caused by a leaper falling across the back of a man who faked him into a jump is a sad spectacle to behold. We try to discourage jumping, except when the offensive man is definitely committed, with his dribble completed.

In our Regional Tournament game with Creighton in 1962 Paul Hogue and George Wilson blocked the first three shots attempted by Creighton's tall and talented Paul Silas. Each block was an example of perfect anticipation of the moves of an opponent. Over the season Hogue was credited with blocking 62 shots, proof that knowledge and anticipation of an opponent's moves are important.

Converting

The real moment of truth in basketball occurs when the offense changes to defense, or *vice versa*. In this chapter, since I am concerned with individual defensive play, I will confine the discussion to the problem of changing from an offensive player to a defensive player with the ball in play. This change takes place in one of two ways: either the opposing team gets a rebound off its defensive board, or you lose the ball on a turnover. In an instant each individual player on your team must convert from offense to defense. It is often in this instant that points are given away.

Playing man-to-man defense, as we do at Cincinnati, means that each player has an assigned man to guard. In the confusion of conversion, however, there is seldom time to sort out the opposing team and pick up the correct man. At such moments our players know that they are to pick up the *nearest* man, apply their usual harassing tactics, force a slowdown in play, and, when it is safe to do so, switch off to the assigned men.

INDIVIDUAL PRESSURE DEFENSE

Converting problems can be stopped or made less dangerous by working on the factors listed here.

1. Tie up the rebounder.
2. Prevent the outlet pass.
3. Send additional men to the board on offense and get the rebound yourself.
4. Get all five men back quickly, even your big men. Run! But don't retreat all the way to your own basket before picking up the nearest man.
5. LET NO MAN GET BEHIND YOU.

In the semi-final game of the 1962 NCAA Tournament, U.C.L.A. gave us the scare of the season during these moments of conversion. A fast team, they dropped all five men back to the defensive board to grab off the rebounds. They then exploded out of the jam under the basket, all five men blazing upcourt at once. Only the tremendous efforts of our players in picking up men and slowing them down kept them from running us right off the court. This U.C.L.A. maneuver, coupled with a fantastic shooting average, turned the game into a seesaw battle that was in doubt until the final six seconds. This was probably the epitome of conversion confusion, but it points up some pertinent facts. Picking up the nearest man is absolutely vital. Informing your teammates of the man you have picked up is necessary, lest two of you go after the same man and leave somebody else free. Lastly, slowing down the action as quickly as possible means that you can get back on your assigned man that much sooner. Otherwise, guards may be left guarding much taller men, or your center may find himself matched with a speedy little guard who can outrun him. Quick pressure on the man with the ball is required.

Best defensive strategy of all, of course, would be to minimize the number of turnovers and lost rebounds. Your opponents cannot score when you have the ball.

One final word about conversion seems called for. If an individual defensive man is outside and finds himself caught by a fast break, he has to be prepared to back-pedal and guard the middle of the foul lane. A true fast break finishes in the middle, remember, and that is where you defend against it.

If I had to summarize the attitude and the skill required to make a great defensive basketball player, I think I would put it all into one sentence. Someone once asked me why Tony Yates plays with a smile on his face, and I answered with these words: "He likes his work." In short, you have to enjoy defense to make it effective. Or, in that one sentence I promised: A great defensive player is not different from other players, he merely does the things they do *more often, harder, and with more pride.*

At Cincinnati we use an assigned man-to-man defense, tailored to Hank Iba's "swinging gate" theory. Iba's Oklahoma State teams first popularized the man-to-man defense with the zone principle. In plain English this means that the defensive men on the ball side play tight, while the defensive men on the side opposite the ball drop off their men, or loosen up, so as to be in position to lend help in the middle.

Assigned man-to-man is the most efficient of all defenses, if it is played correctly. The first requirement is that all five men realize that no individual can let up on his opponent without weakening the entire team effort. In this type of defense the chain is only as strong as its weakest link, and this fact must become a part of every player's mental attitude toward his defensive assignment. Every player must understand his own responsibility in the defensive situation; he must *want* to play man-to-man, because the tremendous demands on his physical stamina cannot be met unless he has the desire to meet his opponent individual to individual, skill against skill, strength against strength—and beat him.

Assigned man-to-man requires every player to give a one hundred per cent defensive effort every second that the opposition has the ball. To be effective, assigned man-to-man defense, as played by Cincinnati, must keep maximum pressure on the offensive team at all times. No offensive player should be able to relax, with or without

4

TEAM DEFENSE

the ball, but should, instead, be subjected to such constant harassment that he is forced into mistakes.

Let us understand right now that pressure defense such as this cannot be taught any more than a goal-line stand in football can be taught. Both are a product of desire, the one magic element in athletics that makes champions. A coaching staff can teach fundamentals of defense and drill a team thoroughly against all kinds of offensive maneuvers, but a coaching staff cannot teach a basketball team to hold a major opponent for fourteen minutes and twenty seconds without a field goal, as the 1961-62 Cincinnati man-to-man defense did. Nor can a coach instruct his team to hold three consecutive teams in one week to 46 *points apiece* in the fierce competition of (1) a playoff game for the conference championship, and (2) two consecutive NCAA Tournament games. Desire, assisted by strict attention to fundamentals, produces such inspired performances.

In this chapter I will examine the fundamental factors of team play responsible for good man-to-man defense; I will not try to find a formula for desire.

The Switch

During our early practices we do not allow our players to switch on defense. We do not want anyone to get in the habit of taking the easy way out in any defensive situation, so at first we encourage every man who is picked or screened to fight over the screen, slide through, roll off —anything short of fouling—in an effort to stay with his assigned man.

As we approach the opening of the season the team is strong enough offensively to make defensive guard play, without switching, almost impossible. Now we permit guards to switch with guards, if such a switch is necessary in order to keep pressure on the offense. This is as far as we wish to go in allowing a switch. Our instructions for the season now are, "Guards switch with guards, if need be. Guards switch with forwards only as a last resort." The players are made to realize that a switch by a guard and forward is an admission of a defensive mistake. Since mistakes will be made, these switches will have to be made, but this cannot be allowed to become a part of our defense.

Since a major factor in our own offense is *taking advantage of defensive switches,* our players are well acquainted with the danger of switching. Most of our basic offensive plays are designed to force a switch. Our team sees these plays work every day in practice and in every game. As a result, our players do not want to switch if it can be avoided. And when it cannot be avoided, they are determined to make the switch a good one, instead of leaving us open for a score by the opposition.

There are two important techniques to remember in making an effective switch. The first is the vocal signal, and the second is what we call the "step out."

The vocal signal to switch is made by the back man, since he is in position to see the pick or screen developing. Almost all teams use the call "Switch!" as a signal. On this call the two defensive men involved in the action are required to switch the men they are guarding. We insist that this vocal signal be given only when the back man is convinced that his teammate cannot fight over or slide through. If possible, the back man should alert his teammate to the developing pick or screen. This is an absolute necessity on a "blind pick" in which the front man is unaware that his backward movement is carrying him directly into a collision with an offensive player. (It is this "blind pick" that usually forces a guard-forward switch, so we want our forwards to shout "Pick! Pick!" when they see this situation, thus alerting the front man and giving him an opportunity to avoid the pick and stay with his man.)

When a switch becomes necessary, the back man must "step out" to pick up his new man. This is vital. The back man cannot merely slide sideways, but must step forward to be on his man tightly as soon as the switch is made. The "step out" technique has to be practiced until it is automatic; it is one of those details that make a difference between good defense and poor defense.

Special situations will arise that call for switching men, even though no picking or screening is involved in the action. On the cut-behind, when one guard allows his man to get past him, we expect the other guard to take that man, if at all possible. The first guard must then quickly switch off to his benefactor's man.

Finally, when our guards trap the man with the ball, the forward who is on the side where there is a free man must come out and cover that man, preventing a pass to him.

Trapping

Trapping, or double-teaming, the man with the ball in order to steal the ball or force a held-ball jump, requires team coördination. Normally, although we play an aggressive, pressure defense, we do not play to steal the ball. We will trap at anytime, however, when the offense tells us to. They may invite the trap in several ways.

1. By crossing guards as they bring the ball up, or move it to set up a play.
2. By allowing one guard to get ahead of the imaginary "line of the ball" as the guards bring the ball up.
3. By taking awkward positions from which a pass would be difficult.

Once invited, we accept with alacrity. Our guards converge on the man with the ball and try to tie him up or steal the ball. The forward opposite the ball comes out to cover the free offensive guard, and the forward on the side of the ball immediately plays in front of his man. Our center is instructed to zone, thereby protecting the basket.

Unless this "covering down" is done quickly and efficiently, trapping will be difficult. The two men most likely to receive a pass from the trap (the guard without the ball and the forward on the ball side) are the most dangerous men in this situation; a pass to either one cannot be permitted.

Like all defensive techniques, trapping must be practiced. The danger of fouling the man with the ball is great, especially when the defensive team is trailing in the ball game and desperate to get the ball. In practice sessions the coach must watch for fouling and not let his players get accustomed to the free-swinging, roughhouse tactics that sometimes characterize poorly trained teams.

Sliding Through

In assigned man-to-man defense, as I have stated, switching should be an exception rather than the rule. *Sliding through should be the rule.* This means that whenever the man you are guarding goes between or behind another offensive-defensive pair, you should make every attempt to stay with your own man. The problem that arises, however, is caused by the fact that there are several routes available, and you must make a choice.

We tell our players, "Don't go fourth man." In other words, avoid a situation in which your teammate and his man are between you and your man. We want our players to react in the following manner:

1. When your teammate's man has the ball, and your man goes behind the ball-man, you go between the ball-man and your teammate.

2. When your teammate's man has the ball, and your man goes between the ball-man and your teammate, you go behind your teammate.

3. The defensive man on the ball-man has preference as far as position is concerned. Under no circumstances must you make him "fourth man."

Whenever possible, the man who is sliding through must be assisted by his teammate. If the man sliding through is coming between, a step back by his teammate will help. If he is going behind, then his teammate should tighten up, if there is a chance to do so. Neither man should be afraid to call to his teammate in these situations.

Skill in sliding through will eliminate the switch in a majority of cases, and elimination of the switch is the ideal in man-to-man defense.

Defensive Preparation for a Game

Prior to every game the University of Cincinnati plays, our "red shirt" team is taught the basic offensive patterns of our coming opponent. On the practice floor we match our starting five against "red shirt" players representing their individual opponents and then have the "red shirts" walk through the newly learned patterns. We do this only long enough to give the starting five a look at the moves and passes involved. Walking through a play is an unnatural experience, and too much of it can be harmful.

Once the players begin scrimmaging in earnest, the coaching staff tries to detect any weaknesses in the defensive adjustments that have been planned for the game. Basically our defense remains the same tight, pressure system that it has been in the past, but slight variations are made. Distortions of the offensive pattern may be forced by an over-play here or a sag there. We run through the pattern again, and this time it is stopped. But what about the option? We run through the option. Sometimes the defensive counter that looked good on paper does not work in practice. Sometimes the skill of one of our own players makes further planning for the option unnecessary. Sometimes the "red shirts" run wild, outscoring the starting five, and we know the mistakes that have been made will not be made again during the game.

Once, during the late minutes of a game, our "red shirt" team having been substituted, we ran our opponent's own offense against him. It was a spontaneous demonstration on the part of the "red shirts," illustrative of the pride they felt in their pre-game contribution to the victory. I neither begrudged them this brief period of relaxation, nor felt that it was intended to humiliate our opponent. Without the ability of the often unsung heroes of the bench to learn a new offense before every game, our own defense could not function the way we want it to.

Summary

I once remarked that "defense is 80 per cent of the game." I have read that quote several times since, usually after Cincinnati has held an opponent to a low score. In making the statement I was trying to sum up a good many years of experience, both as a player and as a coach. Over those years I had seen many fine offensive teams defeated because of a "bad night." Every team hits a cold streak at some time during a season, and when that happens, a strong defense is the only saving factor. A team with such a defense does not panic, but knows that it can remain in the game, always close enough to snatch victory from defeat, should the cold hands suddenly get hot again.

Although the zone defense remains popular, especially in high school play, we have not used it at Cincinnati because we feel that our assigned man-to-man is capable of handling all types of offenses at any time during a game. A team using the zone must come out of its formation if it gets behind in a game. Thus, a team using a zone must also learn man-to-man techniques, and any team that must learn two defenses cannot have full confidence in both.

It seems to me that there is a kind of "Maginot Line thinking" that goes with zone defense. When a team organizes its defense around an established and, hopefully, impenetrable formation of players, any penetration of that defense is psychologically damaging. Easy penetration can be demoralizing.

What seems to me to be the outstanding disadvantage of the zone defense, however, has nothing to do with the technical aspect of basketball. In any sport a participant must be given the opportunity to test himself as an individual competitor. Man-to-man defense gives a boy the chance to learn his own limits of endurance and desire under pressure. The loafer and the careless fall by the wayside. And, as the player learns that his limits of endurance and desire can be expanded by hard work, the champion inside him begins to emerge. I have seen it happen in Cincinnati, and I attribute much of our success to that 80 per cent of the game that is man-to-man defense.

There are valuable side-effects that result from assigned man-to-man defense. Team offense is considerably sharpened when it must be run day after day against the harassing, pressure tactics that are our defensive trademark. Players like Larry Elsasser and Jim Calhoun on our 1961-62 squad forced the starting guards to extend themselves in every practice because they never let up in scrimmages. All players benefited, and all players felt that they had contributed to the team, whether they started a game or not.

A large measure of the success achieved by the offense I am going to describe in the following chapters was due to the excellent defense that faced it during practice sessions.

The team that controls the boards generally wins the ball game. This is not an original observation, of course, but like all the self-evident truths of basketball it bears repeating—again and again and again. Percentagewise, the team that is able to limit its opponents to one shot on each attack, while gaining second, third, and even fourth efforts on its own attack, is a team that is going to win consistently. Since consistent winning is the goal of every coach, rebounding cannot be treated haphazardly; it is an art and a science, as are all phases of the game.

There are two aspects of rebounding, one defensive and one offensive, and they must be treated separately. On the defensive boards the idea is to limit your opponent to a single shot. On the offensive boards the idea is to retain possession for continued effort, or to make another scoring effort by a tip-in.

The Defensive Rebound

The men on the ball-side, usually the center and a forward, should be playing close enough to their men to make contact. This follows the general defensive strategy of playing tight on the ball-side and loose opposite the ball. When the shot is taken these defensive men on the ball-side must feel their opponents; to lose your man at this moment is fatal. Above all, these defensive men *must not watch the ball in flight.* They must

5
REBOUNDING

check their men first, then the ball.

Since most shots are taken from the side, the baseline area is the most likely rebound area. Protection of the baseline area is the first consideration of the front men. They must be alert to rolls or spins by their opponents, and they should be prepared to ride their men hard and long. "Riding a man" means moving with him, keeping tight on him, and maintaining good position. Riding a man hard should bring you into position to box him out. In other words, you should be able to pivot, take a fairly wide stance with your arms and elbows held high, and prevent your man from breaking into the rebound area. Under no circumstances should you back into him, however, or hold him.

The forward opposite the ball has a more difficult time of it because he is playing his man loose. When the shot is taken this forward should open up his stance so that he can see both his man and the ball at the same time. If the offensive man goes baseline, the forward should pivot back on his baseline foot and swing the other leg back to bring himself into proper position. This reverse pivot should gain contact with the offensive man. The object is to bring yourself into a proper boxing-out stance between your man and the ball.

The defensive guards, in our system of play, have a responsibility for defensive rebounding. They must take care of their men, using boxing-out techniques, to prevent these men from going to the boards and assisting there. Far too many teams neglect this guard responsibility because they are more interested in getting their guards to the sidelines for the outlet pass that will start a fast break. It seems more sensible to us to increase our chances of getting possession of the ball in the first place. Since a great many modern teams now send at least one guard in to the offensive board, we feel that it is more important for our defensive guards to keep their men out or go in with them than it is to go running to the sideline for a pass that probably won't ever be thrown. Consequently, we seldom fast break unless the opportunity is simply too good to miss.

The defensive rebounder should gain good possession. We discourage volleyball taps, leaving such maneuvers to the run-shoot-run teams. Our players are instructed to go up for the rebound, to gain possession, to keep the ball high, and to keep the legs spread to clear out the landing field. Elbows are spread, too, but flailing the elbows has been outlawed.

Since referees allow more contact than usual during rebound action, strength and aggressiveness are necessary on the boards. But strength and aggressiveness alone will not suffice. Technique is all important, if you are to gain possession of many defensive rebounds. For emphasis, let me review the procedures that should be followed when your opponent takes a shot.

1. Keep your eyes on your man.
2. Gain contact and then look for the ball.
3. Ride herd on a man who rolls off or spins.
4. Box out.
5. Protect the baseline.
6. Never neglect the offensive guards.
7. Gain possession of the ball before starting your offense.

The Offensive Rebound

"Fire and fall back" may be effective strategy for a retreating army, but using such a strategy in basketball will soon put you out of business. Strangely enough, there are some boys, and sometimes even whole teams, that are satisfied to take one shot and go scuttling back on defense. This is carrying defensive thinking to the point of defeatism.

Second, third, and fourth efforts win games, and even championships. The problem, of course, is how to make certain you get additional chances at the basket on the offensive boards. After watching our second National Championship Team at Cincinnati gain a total of 1536 rebounds during the 1961-62 season, I think I can answer that there is no easy way. Offensive rebounding is a matter of sheer determination. The secret is in working for position by rolling, spinning, sliding or knifing through, and battling your defensive man every inch of the way.

We teach our players to go baseline, using every bit of speed and skill they possess to beat their defensive men. Against a fast-breaking team we send a guard sneaking in, knowing that his defensive man will be more concerned with the outlet pass than with rebounding. Larry Shingleton, the smallest player on our 1961-62 squad at 5' 10", grabbed off 34 rebounds playing the equivalent of one-third of the season. In round numbers that averages out to more than 100 rebounds for a full season, for a "watch charm" guard sifting through giants. Never underestimate the importance of a guard in any phase of the game, and especially in rebounding. The best defense against the fast break is a score; if you have to send one or both offensive guards to the boards to gain additional scoring efforts, accept the challenge. You will be following one of the major trends in present-day basketball if you do.

AN EXPLANATION OF THE DIAGRAMS

The diagrams that follow have been drawn with clarity in mind. In most cases the offensive team has been identified by letters, and the defensive team by numbers, in an attempt to show the normal positions of the offensive players. (F for forward, P for pivot, etc.)

The usual method of identifying the Strong Side and Weak Side of the court by position of the ball *has not been followed,* for the following reasons:

NOTE: Modern offenses depend to a great extent on an overload of one side of the court, since the three-second rule in the foul lane forces the strength of an offense to one side or the other. In the diagrams in which letters are used, therefore, the designation "Strong Side" refers to the overloaded side in the original development of a play.

Whenever it has seemed necessary to use the customary (O) and (X) symbols to represent players, I have identified them as offensive or defensive in the text.

The backbone of our offensive attack at the University of Cincinnati is our Swing-and-Go series. This pattern and its options evolved from our feeling that the one-on-one situation is highly overrated. Most boys are limited in their natural ability to fake and shoot, which means that the old-fashioned system of sticking the forwards far outside and expecting them to score on the one-on-one is a poor gamble. We prefer to set our players up so they can shoot from well-screened or wide-open positions. Our primary purpose in the Swing-and-Go is to force a switch, freeing our pivot man for a lay-up or close shot. You will notice, however, as this series evolves in the diagrams, that no matter which way the defense commits itself, we have an option that gives us a good screen or an open shot.

I got the germ of this offensive idea watching the professionals roll off a double screen. As far as I know, no other team has an offensive pattern similar to this one. It has proved tremendously successful in our games, and its sheer simplicity makes it almost impossible to stop, if opposed by a man-to-man defense.

Theory

In the Swing-and-Go the Strong Side Forward and

6

CINCINNATI'S UNIQUE SWING-AND-GO OFFENSE

the Pivot Man operate as a team only a few steps apart. Since the success of the basic pattern depends upon their reacting together to defensive commitments, it is important that these two men know each other's personal moves as thoroughly as possible. This calls for a great deal of practice together to perfect the timing and screening needed to make this attack work. All shots out of the basic pattern fulfill our demand for close-in shooting.

Basic Pattern

The Swing-and-Go may be set up on either side of the foul lane, although we prefer the left side for a right-handed Pivot Man. Going into the pattern the Pivot Man takes a low post position, and the Strong Side Forward takes a position several steps behind him (as shown in *Diagram 4*). We allow the forward to adjust his position according to the situation; that is, he may move a step or two to the side. He must remain behind the Pivot Man, however, to set up the play.

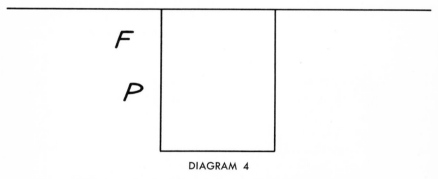

DIAGRAM 4

Positions of forward and pivot in the Swing-and-Go pattern.

In order to receive the ball from the Strong Side Guard, F must free himself from his defensive man by faking. In Diagram 6-2 we show F's fake to take his man as deep as possible, and then his "swing" back over P. If F's defensive man is playing loose, F can swing back without effort. If his man is playing tight, F must be able to maneuver him in.

F's position when he receives the pass from G should be in front of the Pivot Man, although a position to the side of P will suffice. The pass is of primary importance. F must receive the ball at the end of his swing, then turn and immediately face the basket without using his dribble. His next move is determined by the defense. If his man does not follow him

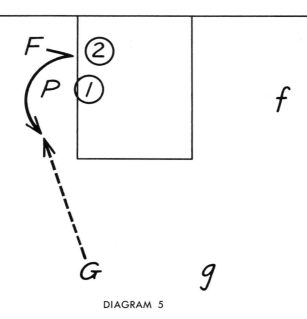

DIAGRAM 5

F drives his man in, then swings off P for the pass from G.

out, he is open for a good shot from where he is. It is surprising how often this simple shot can be taken, especially when *F*'s defensive man is playing loose and finds himself screened out of the play by *P* and *P*'s defensive man.

In most cases, however, *F*'s defensive man will fight through or work for position by going over the top of *P*. In these cases *F* reacts by driving to his left, aided by a pick set up by *P* (as shown in *Diagram 6*). *This is the move that is designed to force a switch by the two defensive men involved.* If the switch is not made, *F* continues his drive for an easy shot.

It is important to note here that *P* must be prepared to set up his pick-screen in two ways. If defensive man No. 2 is in front of him, *P* uses a front pivot. If No. 2 is beside him, *P* uses a reverse or back pivot. In both cases the right foot is the pivoting foot. (These pivots are diagrammed at the end of this chapter.) Again I want to emphasize that these moves are reactions to the defense and must be practiced until they become habits. The man who has to stop and think which way he should pivot will not need to pivot at all, unless he wants to look like a dancer without a partner.

Let us assume that the pick is made cleanly, and that as *F* is driving to his left (*Diagram 6*) defensive men No. 1 and No. 2 switch. *This is*

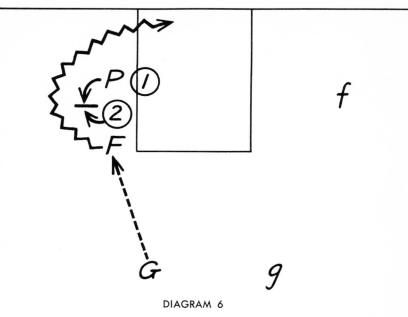

DIAGRAM 6

The defensive man on F (No. 2), has fought through or over the top. F drives to his left and P picks No. 2.

the defensive move that we are trying to force. At the instant of switching the defense is helpless. At that instant P rolls to the basket, takes a pass from *F,* and takes a lay-up. This play is our first choice off the Swing-and-Go pattern because, if the defensive men do their jobs perfectly, we score. *Diagram 7* illustrates this option, which we consider the most powerful weapon in our offensive arsenal.

At every step of this series, the defense will dictate our offensive option. For example, the man on P (No. 1 in *Diagram 7*) may fake the switch and still guard P. That is, No. 1 comes out a step toward F, extending a hand, but he does not pick up F as we wish him to. In this case F does not continue his drive, but takes a close-in shot from the side.

The swing-man, F, must be prepared for one other possibility; namely, a poor defensive reaction to his swing off the Pivot Man at the beginning of the play. If the defensive man on F is late or partially picked as F comes around for the ball, F may elect to drive on around to the foul line and either shoot from there or continue dribbling down the center to the basket. *Diagram 8* illustrates this option.

If F's drive down the center forces a switch by the defensive men, P rolls automatically, and the two-on-one situation pictured in *Diagram 9* results.

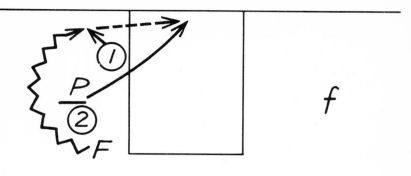

DIAGRAM 7

As F drives to his left, No. 1 and No. 2 switch. On the switch, P immediately rolls to the basket, takes a pass from F, and scores.

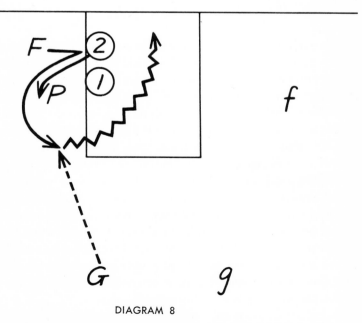

DIAGRAM 8

No. 2 reacts late, or is partially picked. F elects to drive around and down the center. If No. 1 switches off to F to prevent this drive, P will roll to the basket and be free for a pass and shot.

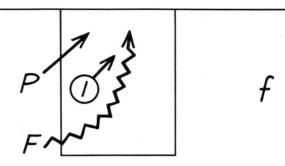

f

9

DIAGRAM 9

No. 1 switches after F starts his drive. P rolls to the basket, setting up a quick two-on-one situation.

The success of our Swing-and-Go depends on the Weak Side Forward's keeping his man busy. If this defensive man is allowed to sag off, he will interfere with the play. To combat this, we tell our Weak Side Forward to interchange with the Weak Side Guard or move to the foul line when F starts his drive *outside*. In running a pattern offense it is always necessary for the offensive men not directly involved with the ball to have definite assignments that will keep them and their defensive men clear of the play.

Although it is possible for both the Strong Side Guard and the Weak Side Guard to make the original pass to the swing-man, F, as he breaks out over the Pivot Man, we have found a pass from the Strong Side Guard more desirable. In most modern defenses the man on G will drop off whenever the ball is on the weak side, making a pass from the Weak Side Guard to F difficult, if not dangerous. Of course, if G's defensive man still sags excessively even when G has the ball, G must clear out after making the pass to F.

As might be expected, various defenses have been thrown at our

CINCINNATI'S UNIQUE SWING-AND-GO OFFENSE

Swing-and-Go since we started using it, but the only perfect defense I have seen thus far is the one we ran into during our tour of the Philippines in the summer of 1961. I will have more to say about that tour in a later chapter, but it is interesting to note here that our games in the Philippines were played according to Olympic rules on courts with a much wider, oblique three-second lane. The boundaries of this lane kept our Pivot Man and Strong Side Forward so far outside that the Swing-and-Go lost its effectiveness. It's tough to beat a guy who uses a bucket of paint and a brush. We had to win without much help from the Swing-and-Go, and the experience convinced me that I am not going to advocate any rule change that tampers with the present width of the American three-second lane. Not while I have a good Pivot Man, anyway.

Continuity off the Swing-and-Go

No pattern offense can be successful if it is made up of set plays that have to be re-set each time they fail to score. Instead, each play has to be part of a general flowing pattern made up of many plays, each of which evolves from any other.

As I have pointed out, Cincinnati's basic Swing-and-Go is a series of pre-planned reactions to man-to-man defensive commitments. Many opportunities for good, close-in shots open up as we run this one basic pattern, but we cannot restrict ourselves to these opportunities alone. In other words, we cannot isolate any particular series in our offense either from other patterns or from options off the same basic pattern. To do so would result in a kind of stop-and-go basketball that would be slow to play and dreary to watch. As you will see in the next chapter, our Backdoor Trap pattern evolves smoothly from the Swing-and-Go, and *vice versa,* without any break in the offensive action.

Many factors, such as the defensive positions of our opponents or the offensive instincts of our own players, determine when our patterns should be changed. Effective continuity in the Cincinnati attack is, in the main, the responsibility of our two guards. As they bring the ball up the floor, they are in the best position to survey the defense and take advantage of any weaknesses they detect. Since our plays are usually keyed by a pass or a cut, we expect our forwards and pivot man to know where the ball is and to be aware of the relative positions of the other men on the floor.

It is my intention to group together all plays run from the basic Swing-and-Go pattern, but I should like you to keep in mind that at any point in our attack, *before we key one of these plays,* it is possible for us to

ILLUSTRATION IV

Pattern offense frees Larry Shingleton for a one-handed lay-up, disproving the theory that the small man has no place in modern basketball.

break into a new series. With that caution, let us look at some of the continuity we develop directly off the high-low positions of the Pivot Man and Strong Side Forward, since these high-low positions are the foundation of this part of our offense.

Guard Double Screen. We designed this play for two reasons. First, we felt that we needed a good, close scoring opportunity that could be set up in the closing seconds of the first half or at the end of a tight ball game. Second, our philosophy of team scoring dictates that our guards be given a chance to make baskets from within the tight semi-circle in which we do most of our scoring. Never underestimate the importance of providing scoring opportunities for your guards, if you are interested in high team morale.

In setting up this particular play we make use of the fact that the Strong Side Forward and the Pivot Man are only a few steps apart, one behind the other. From these positions it is relatively easy for these men to come together and form a shoulder-to-shoulder screen near the foul lane.

Let us assume that we are nearing the close of the first half, have possession of the ball, and call a time-out. During this time-out we instruct our team to run the Guard Double Screen for a final shot. With time once again in, our guards bring up the ball while the forwards and pivot man go into their Swing-and-Go positions. The guards come across the center line, and the ball is worked to the strong side. Now! . . .

The Weak Side Forward keys the play by driving to the foul line for a pass from the Strong Side Guard. The defensive man on the Weak Side Guard must glance at the action to his right because it is his responsibility to know where the ball is going, but that glance or look or peek is also an instant of diversion. In that instant the Weak Side Guard is gone, cutting outside the Weak Side Forward (as shown in *Diagram 10*) and continuing on and around behind the shoulder-to-shoulder double screen set up by F and P. The Weak Side Forward takes one or two dribbles to his right to get the angle for his pass and then passes in to the Weak Side Guard. Up and—we hope—in!

This Guard Double Screen is what we call a "bang-bang" play. It breaks fast, and its success depends upon the timing of the cuts and passes. Like all set plays, however, it must be flexible enough to meet various defensive moves. Although our primary aim is to shoot from behind the double screen, I will illustrate various options that we use off this single situation.

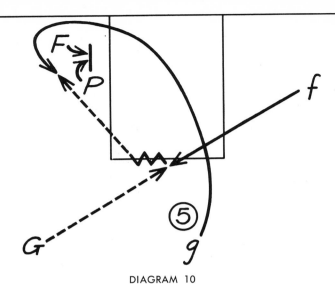

DIAGRAM 10

Guard Double Screen. Here f keys play by going to foul line for a pass from G. When No. 5 looks, g cuts outside f and circles behind the *FP* double screen. f dribbles to right, then passes in to g.

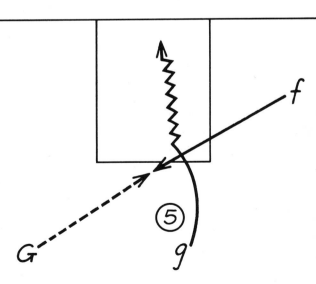

DIAGRAM 11

Option. *Weak Side Guard Play.* Handoff from f to g, who drives in for lay-up.

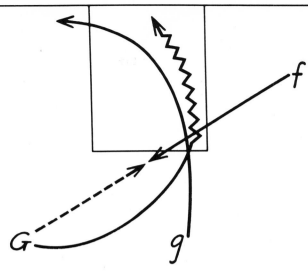

DIAGRAM 12

Option. *Second Guard Around.* Handoff from f to g is faked, and f gives to G who follows g around and drives in for lay-up.

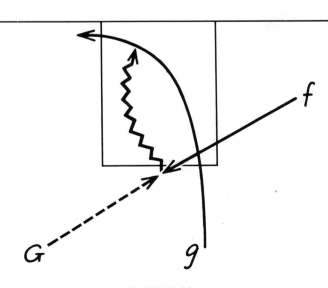

DIAGRAM 13

Option. *Keeper Play.* f fakes handoff to g, then rolls and drives in for lay-up.

CINCINNATI'S UNIQUE SWING-AND-GO OFFENSE

Since the key to the Guard Double Screen and its options is not the pass but *f*'s drive to the foul line, the Weak Side Guard breaks outside *f* even if the ball is not passed from *G* to *f*. If *G* is forced to hold the ball because he cannot get a pass through, then it is his responsibility to feed the ball to *g* behind the double screen. *G* must also be alert to a breakthrough by the defense against the screen. Since such a breakthrough by the man on *P* or the man on *F* actually constitutes a switch, *P* or *F* will roll on the switch and possibly be open for a pass down the middle from *G*.

Forward Double Screen. To take further advantage of the high-low positions of *F* and *P*, we have a second set play designed to score in the closing seconds of a half. Again, the Strong Side Forward and the Pivot Man go into a shoulder-to-shoulder double screen as the play is keyed, and again, as the play develops, these two men are prepared to roll to the basket if their defensive men prove strong enough to break through or over the top of the screen. This much of the pattern is identical to the Guard Double Screen just described, but here the similarity ends.

For our Forward Double Screen the guards work the ball to the weak side, and the play unfolds as follows: The Weak Side Guard, *g*, passes to the Weak Side Forward, *f*, and then follows the ball by moving outside *f*. Here *g* stops and takes a return pass from *f*. *This return pass is the key.*

The instant *f* passes back to *g*, *f* breaks for the basket and continues on around behind the *FP* screen. Possibly dribbling once to free himself, *g* passes across and deep to *G* who passes in to *f* behind the screen (as shown in *Diagram 14*).

We feel that it is important to have plays of this nature in our repertoire. With seconds to go in a tight ball game every man on the team needs to know exactly what is expected of him. This is no time to be making up plays in the huddle, or experimenting out on the floor. In such moments of crisis—and there are many of them during a basketball season—there is no substitute for a well-drilled, well-timed set play. Watching such a play work is one of the real rewards of coaching; making it work is one of the real rewards of playing.

Except for the possibility that a strong defensive man may break through or over the screen, there are no other shot options on this particular play. We do instruct our guards, however, to be careful of the long pass from *g* to *G*. Should *G*'s defensive man be overplaying, making the pass difficult, *G* is instructed to drive across the foul line and toward

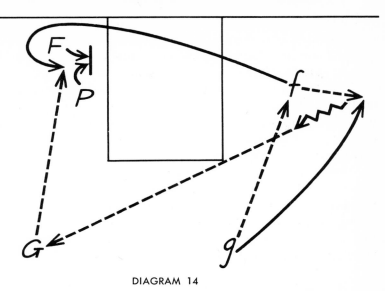

DIAGRAM 14

Forward Double Screen. Pass is made from g to f. g follows ball, going outside. f makes return pass to g and circles behind FP screen. g dribbles free and passes to G, who feeds f behind the screen for a shot.

the weak side corner to clear his man. In this case g must continue his dribble out to the front court and make the feed pass to f behind the screen.

I should like to point out here—especially for the benefit of high school players and their coaches—that the dribble is offensive ammunition; it should be used for a definite purpose within the offensive pattern. The pass is the most effective and quickest way to move the ball, and the fewer passes necessary to set up a shot, the better. We strive for a minimum number of passes in setting up a shot, and we try to train our players to *respect the dribble,* save it for an emergency, and eliminate it whenever possible.

The Five Play. Because the Cincinnati offense gives our guards little opportunity to score from outside, percentages being against long shots off a one-on-one situation, we use plays that bring a guard in for a close shot during our regular attack. (I use the word "regular" here to differentiate between normal floor action and the special spot plays like the Guard Double Screen and the Forward Double Screen.) Too often, normal floor action relegates the guard to a secondary status as far as shooting is concerned, and no amount of flattery about "quarterbacking" and "playmaking" and "feeding" changes the fact that in such offenses the guard is a last, desperate resort when all else fails. At Cincinnati, however, we like happy guards, and happy guards are those who participate in the scoring.

Our Five Play is designed to work the Strong Side Guard to a spot on the baseline halfway between the foul lane and the sideline. This play begins with our men in the Swing-and-Go positions and the ball in possession of the Strong Side Guard. The Strong Side Forward keys the play by moving outside to the extended foul line instead of swinging off the Pivot Man. G passes to F as soon as F reaches his new position. F passes in to the Pivot Man and immediately breaks toward the center to pick G's defensive man. G cuts around the outside of F and drives to his spot on the baseline, where he receives a pass from P and takes a short shot. *Diagram 15* illustrates this play and the manner in which it takes G out of a congested area into a cleared area for his shot.

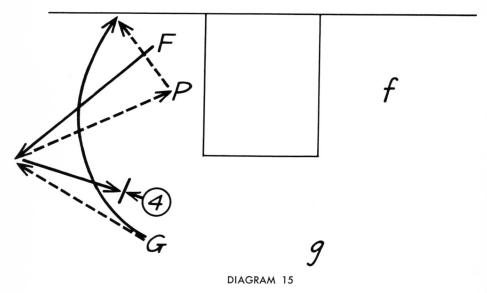

DIAGRAM 15

The Five Play. F breaks to extended foul line and takes pass from G. F passes to P and then cuts to center to pick No. 4, as G cuts outside. P passes to G who shoots from cleared area.

There are two important points I wish to stress here. First, it is necessary for F to cut first (before G) after his pass is made in to the Pivot Man. G cannot break clear until F is in position to screen No. 4 defensive man out of the play. Second, F's first move is to the *extended foul line,* no more and no less. For some reason, the defensive man on *P* will invariably be caught on the wrong side when *F* moves to this position. I cannot explain why this happens, but it does. As a result of this lapse, our forwards are trained to keep the extended foul line in mind whenever a play calls for a pass in from forward to pivot.

While the Five Play is developing, the Weak Side Forward and Weak Side Guard must keep their defensive men occupied, either by interchanging positions or by moving opposite the ball. These two men are called our "play finishers." The Weak Side Forward, especially, is responsible for rebounding, and he is forearmed with the knowledge of exactly where the shot will come from.

I should add, also, that we run this play from either side, on the assumption, naturally, that two happy guards are better than one.

Fake Screen. Quite often we run into opponents whose defensive philosophy is similar to ours. They like to put pressure on right from the start, hoping to force us into mistakes. Since our offense, like all offenses, operates best against a normal defense, we must have methods for keeping the defense "honest," or in normal position.

One of our best methods is a simple little quick opener (shown in *Diagram 16*). This is a fast, effective surprise play that we break off our Swing-and-Go pattern. St. Bonaventure used to use a give-and-go very similar to this quite successfully, although they used it off a different basic series.

We begin the play with a pass from the Weak Side Guard to the Weak Side Forward. The Weak Side Guard then breaks toward the defensive man on the Strong Side Guard as if to screen or pick him, then cuts abruptly down the center and takes a return pass from the Weak Side Forward. When executed correctly, this play has the chastening effect on the defense that we are hoping for. It seems like such an easy way to score. Actually, however, the timing of the Weak Side Guard has to be near-perfect to get this effect. He has to fake his screen in such a manner that the defensive men will react by switching, yet he must not allow them time to switch.

I shall attempt to explain this timing to you.

There is a vulnerable split-second, just before a switch is made, when the offensive men belong to neither defensive man. The body cannot react as quickly as the brain, of course, and though the brain orders, "Switch," the body finds itself caught in a kind of defensive vacuum as it leaves one offensive man for the other, yet is covering neither. An experienced offensive player can sense this instant. The Weak Side Guard must detect it and make his cut between the two closing defenders in that one fraction of time. Run in this manner, the Fake Screen can be devastating.

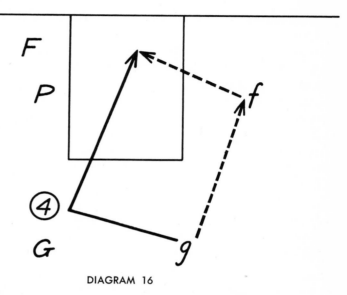

DIAGRAM 16

Fake Screen. With ball on weak side, *g* passes to *f* and then fakes screen on No. 4. *g* drives down center after fake and takes return pass from *f*.

The Seven Play. Miami University of Ohio, our close neighbor to the north, came down to Cincinnati early in the 1960-61 season and gave us a terrific battle. At that time we were beginning to expand our basic patterns, and I was interested in plays that spread offensive power over the whole team, especially plays that involved scoring by the guards. I was particularly impressed by one Miami play that scored three times against us. After studying our films of the game and making the slight adjustments necessary to fit it into our own system, I borrowed the play. At practice we still call it the "Miami play," and we have used it with a good deal of success on many occasions. There ought to be some dramatic reason why we finally adopted the name Seven Play, but, if so, it escapes me. Usually we identify a play with a descriptive name that will tell the players something about its primary objective, but some names seem to evolve by themselves. So Seven Play it is, at least in public, and this is how we work it.

CINCINNATI'S UNIQUE SWING-AND-GO OFFENSE

Coming up on offense we go into our regular Swing-and-Go positions and work the ball to the weak side. The Weak Side Guard passes in to the Weak Side Forward, then cuts inside this forward and drives for the basket, as if to take a return pass. The Weak Side Forward dribbles quickly to the foul line, and the Strong Side Guard then cuts outside him, takes a handoff, and drives in to the basket.

To work this play correctly the Strong Side Guard must set up his man so he can be picked by the Weak Side Forward. We want this guard's defensive man to go with him so that the Weak Side Forward can get at least a piece of him with his pick. Meanwhile, the Weak Side Guard, the first to drive, continues his circle behind the Strong Side Forward and Pivot Man and back out to his normal position.

If the defensive men on the Weak Side Forward and Strong Side Guard switch on the pick, we advise the forward to throw a delayed pass to the Strong Side Guard as his first option.

Notice, in *Diagram 17,* that this play is keyed when the Weak Side Guard makes his cut *inside* the forward.

In running this play, as in running all plays, success depends on timing and execution. An offense is only as good as the sum of all the individual fakes, maneuvers for position, shooting accuracy, and tip-ins that

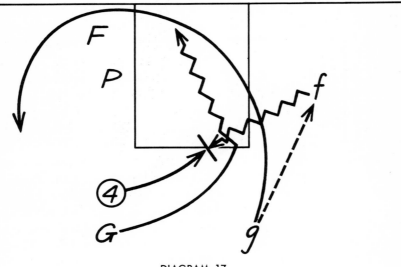

DIAGRAM 17

The Seven Play. With ball on weak side, g passes to f and cuts inside toward basket. f dribbles to foul line, hands off to G who is cutting outside f. As f partially picks or screens No. 4, G drives in for the shot.

59

ILLUSTRATION V

An option off the Swing-and-Go pattern. Ron Bonham takes a jump shot
from behind the pivot man.

make it up. In addition, offensive power increases in direct proportion to the ability of each man to take advantage of unforeseen opportunities. The man with the ball will often observe an opening in the defense that has not been charted into a particular play. He may find a clear path to the basket or a man free to take a quick pass and lay it up. When such unexpected opportunities present themselves, we want them to be exploited. The well-planned and well-drilled plays give cohesion and organization to a pattern offense; the individual capacity for exploiting defensive mistakes gives it excitement.

Clearance Plays. In our Cincinnati offense we follow an unwritten rule that goes something like this: *Clear out men who sag on the pivot.* Since this sagging is done to clog up the area near the pivot, or to double-team him, or to prevent a pass in to him, we try to free him of extra pressure by having our guards or forwards take their men away. We leave such moves up to the individuals on the court, therefore, we cannot design set plays for clearance.

In general, we try to pass the ball to the Pivot Man when his defensive man has two or three personal fouls early in the game, or any time his defensive man accumulates four fouls. Since the defensive man will have to play loose, we feed the Pivot Man as much as possible. At such times, of course, other defensive men will try to sag on our Pivot Man to assist in defending him. Clearing out these helpers is mandatory.

When one of our outside men with the ball sees his pass to the Pivot Man result in a sag by the man guarding him, the outside man knows that he is going to get the ball back immediately from the Pivot Man. This return pass should be automatic and quick. In many cases this quick return pass from the Pivot Man defeats the sagging defensive man long enough for the outside man to get off a shot. "If you expect the ball passed in to you," we tell our Pivot Man, "you have to pass it outside when they're sagging." Otherwise those boys on the outside may get a little unhappy with all that giving and no receiving.

Pivot Screens Used in the Swing-and-Go Series

I pointed out earlier that during the running of the Swing-and-Go series the position of the Strong Side Forward's defensive man dictated whether the Pivot Man used a front pivot or a reverse pivot to set up his screen. Since these pivots are so important to the success of the series, I want to illustrate them. In the diagrams that follow the shaded feet represent the positions of the defensive man who is to be screened, the black foot represents the pivoting foot of the Pivot Man, and the white foot represents his non-pivoting or sliding foot. *Diagrams 18* and *19* show the best pivot reactions when the Strong Side Forward cuts back outside and drives for the basket, while *Diagrams 20* and *21* show the moves to be made when the Strong Side Forward continues his swing around to the foul line.

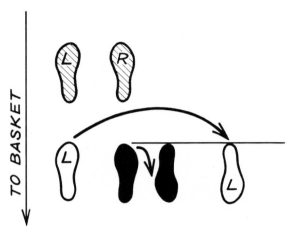

DIAGRAM 18

Front Pivot Screen. Defensive man has broken through or over the top and is in front of Pivot Man. Right foot is pivoting foot.

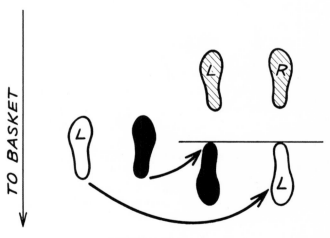

DIAGRAM 19

Reverse Pivot Screen. Defensive man has come over the top and is alongside Pivot Man. Right foot is pivoting foot.

CINCINNATI'S UNIQUE SWING-AND-GO OFFENSE

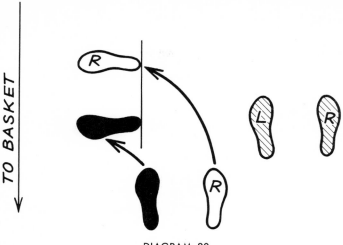

DIAGRAM 20

Front Pivot Screen. Pick set up by Pivot Man when forward goes around toward foul lane and down the center. Left foot is pivoting foot. Used when forward's defensive man is alongside Pivot Man.

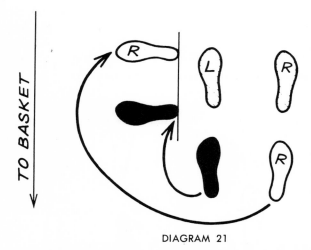

DIAGRAM 21

Reverse Pivot Screen. Pick set up by Pivot Man when forward goes around toward foul lane. Left foot is pivoting foot. Used when defensive man is in front of Pivot Man.

To be effective a pattern offense must consist of several distinctive series which are interchangeable. When the change is made from one series to another, however, no complicated shifting of positions should be involved. These changes are made in the heat of a ball game, remember, and this is not quite the same as making them on the practice floor or on your blackboard.

At Cincinnati we like to have one series flow from another without any change in the tempo or momentum of the offensive attack. The Backdoor Trap series, which I am going to describe in this chapter, is designed to evolve quickly from the Swing-and-Go. It can be transformed back into the Swing-and-Go just as swiftly, as I have illustrated in *Diagram 22*. It is this change from series to series *without hesitation* that keeps the defense off balance. Except for the Strong Side Forward, no one seems to have taken a new position, and yet the whole pattern of the Backdoor series is different from what has preceded it. Thus, just as the defense begins to sense the moves of one series, we casually shift a single player and confront our opponents with a whole new set of passes, cuts, and shots.

Refinements on a Borrowed Pattern

Before I detail our version of the Backdoor Trap, I want to disclaim any credit for originating the basic pattern. Back in 1959 and 1960 Pete Newell and his

PATTERN OFFENSE:
THE BACKDOOR TRAP

great University of California Golden Bears showed us the Back Door in a couple of NCAA Tournament games, and I filed the pattern away for future study. St. Louis University has a modification of this same pattern in the Billiken arsenal, and during the 1961-62 season Ohio

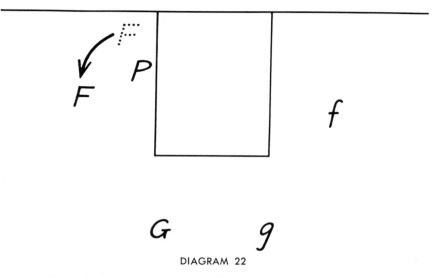

DIAGRAM 22

Positions of offensive players in the Backdoor Trap pattern. Notice that F makes the only change from the Swing-and-Go.

State treated the Big Ten to a variation on the same theme. Versions of this particular series seem to be cropping up on all sides, indicating that it is an extremely effective way to score points.

At Cincinnati we use a refined and reworked California pattern, believing that what works for a Bear should work for a Bearcat as well. Of course, we have developed our own options to fit our own personnel, and the result is a Backdoor series that is, when viewed in its entirety, unlike any other series of the same name.

Theory

Our Backdoor Trap series has one purpose: to give our big men at the forwards and pivot tremendous scoring power in close to the basket. In operation, we swing the Backdoor pattern from side to side, running it from the left and right and left again without pause. The distinctive feature of the basic pattern is this shuttling movement, which alternates forwards and pivot men in their positions as one after the other they break in toward the basket. As in all of our offensive patterns, the Backdoor series is designed to take advantage of defensive commitments and mistakes in close, where mistakes are fatal.

Basic Pattern

The success of the primary play in our Backdoor series depends upon the success of the Strong Side Forward in setting up his man for a pick by the Pivot Man. We want the Strong Side Forward to walk his man back toward the Pivot Man before faking and cutting for the basket. Once the defensive man on the forward commits himself in response to the fake, the forward breaks away from the direction of the commitment. When the play runs perfectly, the Strong Side Forward is able to go baseline, as illustrated in *Diagram 23*. Here I show *F*, starting in his outside position, an indication to the guards that the Backdoor Trap is on. The actual keying of the play, however, is left to *g*, who has the ball. If *g* passes to *f* and then breaks around *f* to the baseline, the play is signaled. *F* must see *g* continue to the baseline before he makes his own move, however. Seeing *g* do this, *F* forces his defensive man back toward *P,* fakes him upcourt, then cuts off *P* and takes a quick pass under the basket from *f*.

In the event the defensive man on *F* cannot be faked away from the

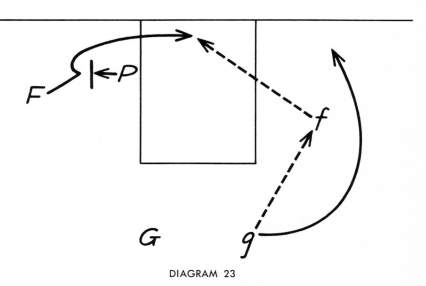

DIAGRAM 23

When *g* passes to *f* and then cuts outside *f* to the baseline, the play is keyed. *F* backs his man into *P's* pick and then cuts off *P* for the pass from *f*.

baseline, F can elect to cut off above P rather than below him. As in all of our plays, our players react to the defensive moves and try to use them to our advantage. No matter which direction the defensive man on F commits himself to, he should be forced into a pick by P, freeing F.

Since no play can be run perfectly every time, there is a chance that f will not be able to make the feed pass in to F. In that event, the players do not stop their movement, but continue into the positions illustrated in *Diagram 24*.

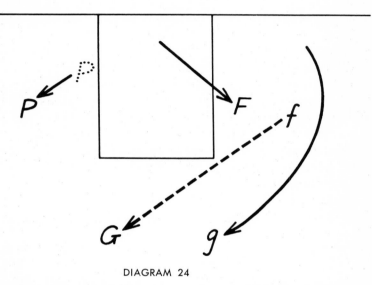

DIAGRAM 24

Backdoor Trap continued. Unable to hit F, f passes out to G. P moves outside to become a forward. g returns to original position.

Study Diagram 24 closely, if you wish to understand the shuttling motion of this series. Notice that F now occupies the pivot position on the opposite side, while f has become the Strong Side Forward, and P has moved out several steps to become the Weak Side Forward. G takes the release pass from f, and we are ready to run the same play from the other side. Meanwhile g is coming back out to his original position, prepared to start the whole thing over again, if the play misses a second time. It will take *six complete shifts* before the offensive men are back in their original positions. Such a variable attack, while simple in operation, can be bewildering to the defense. The quick change of forwards and pivot man, as far as position is concerned, will force a defensive mistake at some time during this cycle of six shifts. The aim of this

ILLUSTRATION VI

Yates, driving in for a one-handed lay-up. "Guards who get to score are happy guards."

pattern is to have one of our big men take advantage of that mistake.

It is important to emphasize that the guard, g, making the first pass and keying the play *must cut to the baseline*. This prevents his defensive man from sagging on f, who has to make the feed pass. In addition, it is up to g to see to it that the defensive man on G does not sag off. We do not want the strong side clogged up by a sagging guard, especially if the situation calls for the Strong Side Forward to cut high instead of going baseline. If g notices that G's defender is sagging, then g passes to G to bring that man out before the play begins. When G makes a return pass, the play can proceed as diagrammed.

Continuity off the Backdoor Trap Pattern

In modifying the Backdoor series for our offense I was convinced that the side-to-side, or shuttle movement of the basic attack would lull the defense into a feeling that they had diagnosed our pattern. Often a basic play will score once or twice before the defenders sense what is happening, but, inevitably, a good team will make defensive adjustments to stop any set pattern. It is always necessary to plan a few surprises and spring them on the opposition as soon as you have them lulled into a sense of security.

Our continuity off the Backdoor Trap pattern contains a good many surprises, all of them possessing good scoring potential. If I were recommending only one part of our total offense to a high school coach, I would choose the Backdoor series for the following reasons:

1. Simplicity of operation combined with a great deal of movement,
2. A shifting of positions that gives the appearance of complexity,
3. A variety of quick, even daring options that players enjoy.

Give-and-Go Down the Middle. Sometimes, as the basic pattern shuttles from side to side, the Weak Side Guard will notice that the defense is beginning to overplay to the outside. This happens when the defender on the Weak Side Guard begins to sense the movement of the play and concludes that his man always cuts *outside* the Weak Side Forward after passing. Against such an overplay the Weak Side Guard passes in to the forward as before, but cuts quickly *down the middle* for a quick return pass and lay-up.

On this option it is extremely important that the Strong Side Forward stay in his original position and forego his cut to the basket; otherwise there will be two offensive men cutting into the same spot at the same time. Our forwards know that they are not to cut to the basket unless the Weak Side Guard goes *outside* the Weak Side Forward *and continues to the baseline*. This is where the patience and discipline gained in practice pay off. A heedless or impatient player who forgets the keys might just as well be playing on the opposing team.

Crosscourt Pass Option. Although the crosscourt pass is considered a cardinal sin of basketball, we employ it deliberately in our Backdoor series. In the diagrams below I have illustrated the development of this play in detail. The play is keyed in the usual way, with g passing to f and then continuing to the baseline. F makes his cut to the basket. Assuming that f cannot feed the ball in to F, we see that F continues across the foul lane to take up a pivot position on the opposite side. P comes out about two steps as indicated in the first diagram, while G moves toward the middle to pull his defensive man away from P, as well as putting himself in position for a release pass from f, if one should be needed.

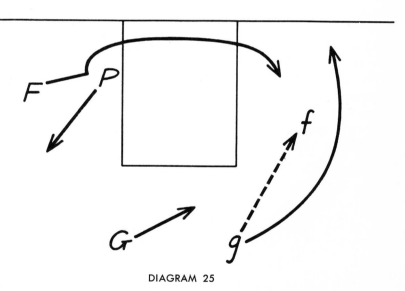

DIAGRAM 25

Option. *Crosscourt Pass,* first movements. Backdoor Trap has been unsuccessful. F becomes pivot man and P becomes forward.

Unable to pass to the cutting F, and alert to P's movement, f throws a quick, hard pass across court to P. P can now drive in for a lay-up, take a jump shot, or feed in to f who is now breaking off F in a continuation of the basic Backdoor Trap. *Diagram 25* illustrates this last option.

PATTERN OFFENSE: THE BACKDOOR TRAP

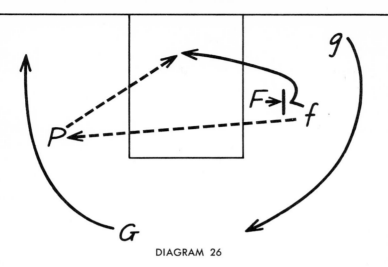

DIAGRAM 26

Crosscourt Pass, concluded. Forward with the ball, *f,* passes to P and immediately breaks off F in new cycle of Backdoor Trap. P can shoot or pass to *f* as shown. G goes to the baseline to help rebound.

Notice that the two guards in *Diagram 26* are responsible for reversing their positions in this particular option.

This play has been quite successful for us, especially at a time when we have a sharpshooter such as Ron Bonham shifted into the pivot spot during our cycle. The pass across court often catches the defensive men with their backs turned, giving P time for his jump shot. At other times the defensive man on P, caught off guard by the pass, will make a lunge upcourt, making it easy for P to fake him out and go on in for the lay-up.

Fake Backdoor Trap. If, after several rotations of the basic pattern the defensive men on P and F begin to anticipate F's cut to the basket, or if our players feel that these men are preparing to switch, we have a quick option that has proved effective time and time again. *Diagram 27* illustrates the simple moves required. The play is keyed as usual, with a pass and cut outside by *g,* but this time the Pivot Man turns quickly and breaks to the basket, taking a quick pass from *f* and laying it up and in. Our great center, Paul Hogue, was especially adept at catching the defense flatfooted on this play because he was deceptively quick in spite of his tremendous size. Striking with surprising suddenness during the shuttling movement of the Backdoor cycle, this particular option can have a demoralizing effect on the defense.

The Okie Play. If anyone needed proof that I have been describing

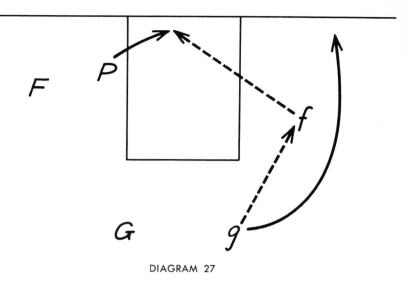

DIAGRAM 27

Option. *Fake Backdoor Trap.* Original pass and cut outside by *g* are the same as Backdoor Trap. *P* turns quickly and breaks to basket, for pass from *f.*

the authentic Cincinnati basketball system in these pages, he would find it in the names of the plays. Our time in skull sessions and practice sessions is spent in perfecting the game of basketball, not inventing fancy names for it. Thus the "Okie Play"—a name whose origin is lost in the dim past of some grueling inter-squad scrimmage, but nevertheless an effective weapon at those times when the defense needs to be kept honest. *Diagrams* 28 and 29 show the two components of this play, starting with *g*'s usual pass to *f* and cut to the baseline, and the resulting break under the basket by *F*. You will notice, however, that *G* now receives a quick pass out from *f*. This pass is a key for *P* to break diagonally to the foul line. *Diagram* 29 continues the action, with *G* dribbling off *P*, trying to force a switch. If the switch is not made, *G* continues his dribble to the basket, as I have shown. If the switch is made, then *P* rolls to the basket, takes a feed pass from *G* and lays it up.

As always, speed and timing are necessary for the success of this option. The ability of *f* in spotting which of the options open to him will prove to be the best cannot be overlooked. What seems easy on paper turns out to be much more difficult on the floor. Coordination and skill come from hours of practice, and a score in our brand of deliberate, pattern basketball comes when all five men carry out their

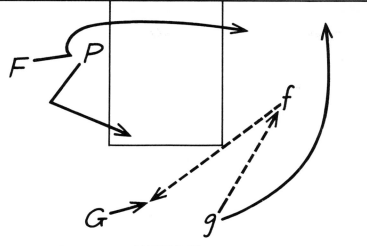

DIAGRAM 28

Option. *The Okie Play,* first movements. g passes to f, but f is unable to get a pass in to the breaking man, *F*. P starts to move outside, but cuts quickly to the foul line when f passes outside to G.

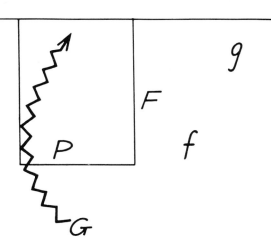

DIAGRAM 29

The Okie Play, concluded. G dribbles off P, trying to force a switch. If switch is made, P rolls to the basket for a pass. If switch is not made, G continues in as shown.

responsibilities to the fullest. So who has time to sit around thinking up names?

Two Double Screens off the Basic Pattern. As I explained in the preceding chapter, we like to set up a double screen when we are coming down to the final moments of a close game. We also like to provide our best shooters with more freedom to take a shot than they would get in a simple one-on-one situation. For these reasons we have added two double screens to our general Backdoor series, one beginning on the weak side and one beginning on the strong side. In *Diagrams* 30 and 31 that follow you will notice that the guards making the initial passes on these two plays do not cut to the baseline. The guard's stopping outside the forward and taking a return pass from the forward *is the key for the double screen.* When the guard stops and takes that return pass, let me repeat, the double screen is on.

Let me add a few words of advice here for the benefit of readers who are planning to put some of the foregoing ideas into their own offense. The last two diagrams point up one of the difficulties of following a play on paper. At first glance both of these double screens seem complex, if not confusing. Walking through the various movements is the only method of clarifying the timing required to make these plays

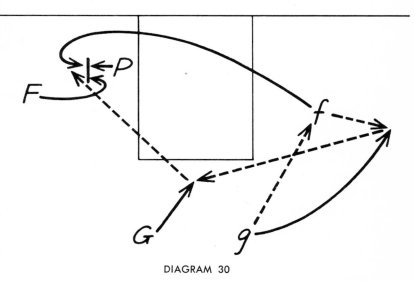

DIAGRAM 30

Forward Double Screen 1. g passes to f then cuts outside f, takes return pass from f. Passes then go from g to G to f who has cut around behind FP double screen.

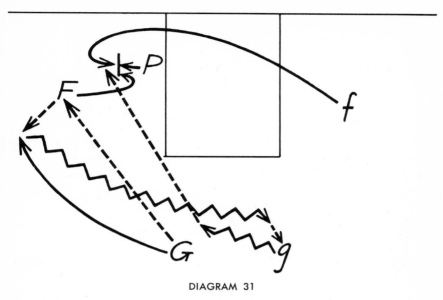

DIAGRAM 31

Forward Double Screen 2. With ball on strong side, G passes to F, then cuts outside F, and takes return pass from F. G dribbles back to middle, gives ball to g, and g feeds f behind the FP double screen.

work. If you ask, for example, "When does *f* break?" I can only reply, "How fast is the man who will be in this position?" Success or failure of any play depends entirely upon the capabilities of the players. My own bookshelves are crowded with volumes full of perfect plays—on paper. I offer you offensive patterns that have worked enough times on the basketball floor to earn two National Championships. They can be made to work, but only after long, hard hours of practice with your own boys in your own gymnasium.

Forward-Guard Interchange. While not a play in itself this maneuver can be effective in confusing the defense. It is simply an interchange of positions by the forwards and the guards during the offensive action described in this chapter. To key or signal this interchange the Pivot Man moves out of his regular Backdoor position to a high post. The guard with the ball immediately passes to the pivot man, who holds the ball until the forwards and guards have switched places, with the forwards moving out to guard positions and the guards moving in to forward positions. The Pivot Man then passes out to one of the outside men, as shown in *Diagram 32*, and moves to a pivot-screen position

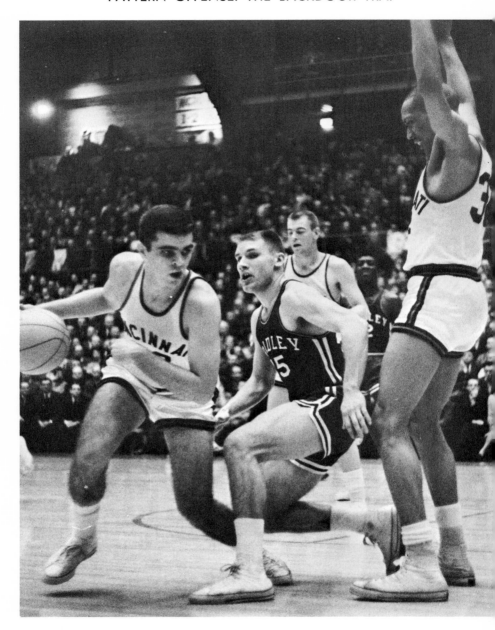

ILLUSTRATION VII

Defensive man caught by a pick. Here the forward is picking for the guard
with the ball, who has set his man up effectively. If this pick forces a switch,
the forward will roll to the basket.

PATTERN OFFENSE: THE BACKDOOR TRAP

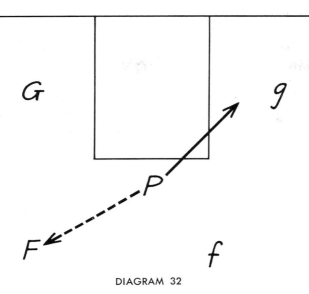

DIAGRAM 32

Forward-Guard Interchange. Pass to P who has moved out to high post is key for this switch of positions. Drawing shows P passing out to F and then going to low post opposite the ball to begin Backdoor series.

opposite the ball. The Backdoor series now unfolds with the guards as front men.

It may be possible for g to cut off P immediately and take a direct pass in from F. If not, then F can start the series in the usual manner. Percentages being what they are, it should not be necessary for me to add that we do not keep our guards playing forward for very long. The odds are still better with the big men up front, but anything that will befuddle the defense, even for one quick play, is worth adding to the offense.

The Backdoor Offense

The series I have presented in this chapter could be utilized as an entire offense. It contains the elements necessary for a strong attack, namely, continuous motion, variation, and surprise. In all, with the six shifts possible in the basic cycle, there are thirty scoring opportunities out of this single pattern, plus the opportunities that arise when the guards and forwards interchange. Against Duquesne during the 1961-62 season we scored three times in a row on the basic pattern alone, and had the cutting forward free under the basket our next time on offense, only to have a slippery ball cause the feed pass to go sailing off into the stands.

Like our Swing-and-Go series, however, the Backdoor series is designed to work against a man-to-man defense. And it is designed to alternate with the Swing-and-Go series at any time, remember, without any change in our tempo. With these two series, and with the series I will describe in the next chapter, our offense has generated scoring power against some of the best teams in modern collegiate basketball.

It should be obvious by now that our offensive power is concentrated on the high-percentage area in close to the basket. In describing the Swing-and-Go pattern and the Backdoor pattern I have explained how this power is developed against a good man-to-man defense. I have not discussed, however, one troublesome possibility that may result from this concentration of shooting in close, namely, the tendency of a top-flight defensive team to sag off on us in an attempt to jam up the middle.

It is no secret to any of our opponents that we are going to play for the good shot, nor is it a secret that congestion around and under the basket will make our job much more difficult. What has been a secret until now is the means by which we combat this tendency to jam our best offensive area with defensive men.

Our antidote is a simple series that we call our High Post, designed to keep the defense honest while we break out a set of quick opening plays from outside. Over the past two years this series has served us well, and I expect it to serve us well in the future. (I am confident my colleagues in collegiate coaching will not believe that I am furnishing them with a more detailed description of the Cincinnati offense than they can ever get from their own scouts, despite the fact that this is exactly what I am doing. It has been my experience in speaking to basketball clinics that no one believes that I only describe what we use, *until I show the movies of*

8

PATTERN OFFENSE: THE HIGH POST

our games.) The skepticism with which certain opponents will greet the descriptions of our High Post series in this present chapter will allow us to get away with it for many seasons to come.

Theory

In our High Post series we operate on the theory that bringing our forwards and center high will force the defense to open up the area near the basket. We also depend on the fact that only rarely will a defensive pivot switch off on a cutting guard because of the danger of leaving a small man to guard the offensive pivot. In addition, we cling to our philosophy that basketball should be a team effort, and we have designed the High Post plays to involve guards, forwards, and pivot in the scoring. We want this pattern and its options to hit fast, with a minimum of passing, and with the attack liable to come from any one of three positions. In short, our wants are simple. Satisfying them, however, requires the same qualities of timing and discipline that characterize our entire system.

Basic Pattern

To begin the High Post series our Pivot Man comes high, just above the middle of the foul line. Both forwards also come high, taking outside positions on the extended foul line. The guards bring the ball into the backcourt and overplay to the side on which the passing will begin. For the purpose of clarity, I will call this side the Strong Side in the descriptions to come. *Diagram 33* illustrates the basic pattern, with the passing scheduled to begin on the right side. Play can also begin to the left, at the discretion of the guards.

The basic play off this pattern calls for the Weak Side Guard to score on a cut down the middle, and it unfolds as illustrated in *Diagram 34*. First the ball is worked to the Strong Side Guard, who keys the play with a pass in to the Strong Side Forward. As this pass is made, the Weak Side Guard, g, drives his defensive man back into the Pivot Man, then cuts off the Pivot Man and continues down the middle to take a quick pass from the Strong Side Forward and lay it up and in.

All that is necessary to make this basic High Post play work is for the defensive man on g to be momentarily picked by the Pivot Man. Speed will free g for the feed pass, if this pick is even slightly successful. As always, g's skill in setting up his man for the pick cannot be over-

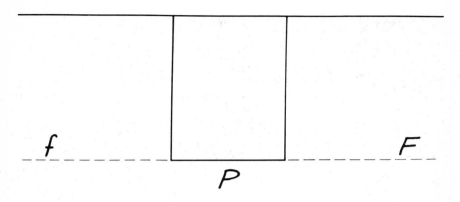

DIAGRAM 33

Positions of offensive players in the High-Post pattern. Note the extended foul line, a key checkpoint for Cincinnati forwards and guards.

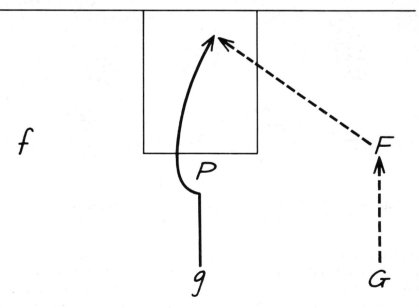

DIAGRAM 34

G passes to F. g cuts off P and takes feed pass from F.

ILLUSTRATION VIII

Guard, Tony Yates, drives off towering Paul Hogue. Pattern offense is designed to bring guards into high-percentage scoring areas.

emphasized. Carl Bouldin, co-captain of our 1960-61 team, made an extraordinary number of baskets on this play because of his ability to take his man into the pick. Bouldin took advantage of his defensive man's tendency to sag on the high Pivot Man. Since, by sagging, the defensive guard was moving himself closer to the pick, Bouldin also moved closer. Often one step and a fake were all that was necessary to drive the defensive man into big Paul Hogue at the pivot. An instant later Bouldin was off for the basket.

On the rare occasions that desperation forced a switch on this particular play, our Pivot Man automatically rolled to the basket and was fed the pass from the Strong Side Forward. Invariably, height won out.

Before continuing with the development of the options on this series, let me explain why we do not discourage sagging on the Pivot Man in this attack. First, as I have pointed out, such sagging works to our advantage when we want to pick the defensive man on the Weak Side Guard. Second, we are attempting to convince our opponents that sagging will get them in trouble, so that they will not get in the habit of sagging off against our Swing-and-Go and Backdoor patterns. Third, and most unusual for a high-post situation, *we never pass in to the Pivot Man on this series.* Unlike some give-and-go, high-post patterns used elsewhere, ours is a series that has the initial pass going away from the Pivot Man. Sagging on him when he is at a high-post position will not hamper our attack because we are not trying to hit him there.

The only time we ever pass to the high post against a man-to-man defense is when we key the forward-guard interchange described in chapter 7.

Continuity off the High Post Series

There are many play possibilities inherent in the basic High Post pattern, but at Cincinnati we do not use this pattern as a major part of our offense. Once it serves its purpose of tightening up the defense, we usually turn on the inside power generated by our other patterns. Up to now I have never felt the necessity of working out a complicated series of options to be run from the original high-post positions. As a result, we run a minimum of quick openers, drill on them until the timing and moves are as near perfect as possible, and let it go at that. The flow from one option to another is difficult from this far outside, since the long drive to the basket takes the man driving or cutting so far from his original position. Also, our rebounding power is scattered on this pattern. Fortunately, these disadvantages are balanced somewhat by the high percentage of baskets we make when we run this series.

Pivot Pick for Forward. Sometimes the Weak Side Guard cutting off the Pivot Man in the basic play of this series cannot shake his man.

Either the man manages to slide through or is fast enough to go over the top of the pick and still ride herd on our guard. In such a situation the Pivot Man must react swiftly by moving to the side, opposite the ball, and screening the Weak Side Forward's defensive man. *Diagram 35* illustrates such a reaction and the resulting play. The Weak Side Forward takes his man several steps toward the basket, then suddenly cuts back over the top of the Pivot Man to the foul line. Here *f* is free for a shot or free to drive to the basket, if the area is clear.

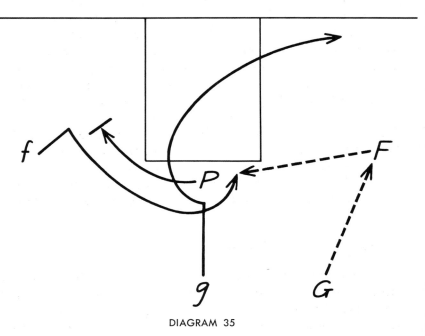

DIAGRAM 35

Pivot Pick for Forward. F is unable to hit g on basic play. P moves to pick f's defensive man, while f fakes and then cuts off P for feed pass from F.

As always, we hope to force a switch when the Pivot Man picks or screens. If the switch is made, we expect the Pivot Man to roll automatically to the basket for a feed pass and lay-up. It is also expected that the Weak Side Guard will continue into the corner when his option fails, thus clearing his man out of the middle.

Nothing fancy unfolds here, you understand. This is straightforward, fundamental basketball, and its success depends entirely on the skill of the individuals. Unless the players are trained to pass effectively, set up their men, react to a switch, and time their movements, nothing will work.

High Post Roll. Here, too, we have a fast and simple play that relies on excellent application of fundamentals for success. Setting up in our High Post pattern, we work the ball to the Strong Side Guard as usual. This time, however, the Weak Side Guard does not cut off the Pivot Man because this would jam up the area where the play will break. Instead, the Strong Side Guard, G, feeds the ball to the Strong Side Forward and then cuts outside the forward, as shown in *Diagram 36.* The Strong Side Forward returns the ball to G and then moves swiftly across the foul lane. The instant F passes, P rolls to the basket off F, takes a quick pass from G, and scores.

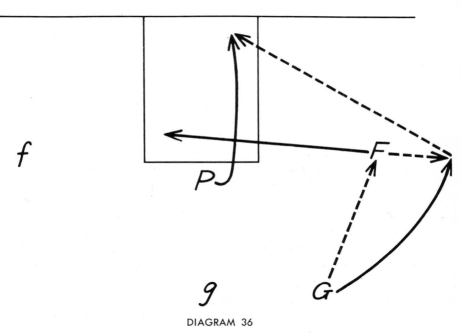

DIAGRAM 36

High Post Roll. G passes to F then cuts outside F for return pass. F breaks across foul lane. P rolls to basket as F goes in front of him. G then passes in to P.

In the event that G is unable to get the ball in to P, we instruct our Pivot Man to go quickly to a low-post position on the ball side. G passes to him here, and then screens for g, who breaks to the baseline for a short feed pass from P, and a close-in jump shot. In essence, this option, illustrated in *Diagram 37,* is a variation of the Five Play described in chapter 6.

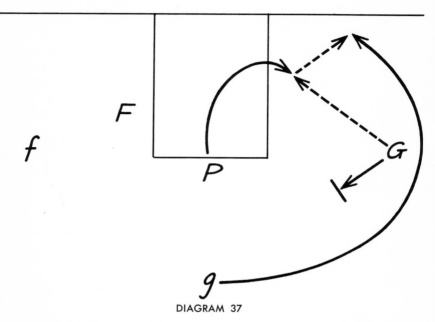

DIAGRAM 37

Option. Five Play off Roll. G is unable to hit P on the High Post Roll. P goes to low post on ball side immediately. G passes to P and then picks for g who cuts outside and deep for short pass from P.

As I pointed out earlier, I have discussed these options off the High Post pattern many times in various clinics throughout the country, and I have been amused by the reactions these discussions provoke. High school coaches, especially, seem to feel that such plays are too simple to be true. National Championships, their reactions seem to say, cannot possibly be won with such basic offensive ammunition. To which I can only reply that the record of the 1960-61 and 1961-62 Cincinnati teams cannot be discounted, if proof is necessary.

Summary

In these three chapters on Pattern Offense I have described the entire Cincinnati system for attacking a man-to-man defense, and I have attempted to explain the philosophy and theories responsible for the development of this system. Throughout this discussion of offensive

ILLUSTRATION IX

Guard, Carl Bouldin, shoots over a screen. Note that the man screening
is beginning to roll to the basket for the rebound while his opponent
watches the ball.

series I have tried to emphasize that basketball is a team game, rather than an exhibition by individual super-stars. By returning the opportunity to score to the entire team, a coach decreases problems of morale and discipline, builds team spirit, and develops in his players an enthusiasm for defense.

In the Swing-and-Go series (chapter 6) I presented an original pattern that has been tested over two seasons of top-flight intercollegiate competition. The Backdoor Trap series (chapter 7) is, in its basic form, one of the most widely used patterns in modern basketball. Our modifications on the Backdoor Trap have succeeded far beyond our first expectations. I suspect that some variation of this pattern will shortly become the Split-T of basketball, finding its way into the offense of most teams, from the collegiate tournament courts to the sandlots. For too long a time offensive basketball has belonged to a few talented individuals, and, while it is only just that such players should receive recognition for their shooting skill, the concentration on scoring records has discouraged many boys from adopting basketball as a sport. By revealing the details of an offense that has been responsible for two successive National Championships I hope to contribute some arguments for team basketball and thus offer some encouragement to any coach and team willing to undertake the training and discipline required to play winning pattern basketball.

There is no easy method of winning ball games. A pattern offense offers no magic formula for success. Instead, the system used by our Cincinnati teams calls for strict attention to details in practice, it calls for hard work, and it calls for desire. We try to leave nothing to chance or to the sudden impulses of a player caught up in the pressures of a game with 15 thousand screaming spectators surrounding him. Our practice drills (chapters 9 and 10) are designed to condition our players to the type of game we play. In practice we develop the reactions that make our players respond automatically to each situation that arises. We practice hard and we scrimmage hard. There are no light workouts, *even on the day before a game.* The idea that a light practice session is necessary the day before a game has somehow become part of modern basketball lore, but it has no place in our training program. A team that "lets down" the day before it is to play must be brought "up" again. Sometimes it takes the whole first half before such a team can regain its peak. By then it is often too late to get back into the ball game. We try to be in the ball game from the first jump, and we feel that a regular practice the preceding day helps put us there.

I have often been quoted as saying that "defense is 80 per cent of the game," but I do not mean to imply by this statement that offense is not important. Given a strong defense, I feel that a flexible pattern offense, such as I have presented, is sufficient to get the job done. It is designed deliberately to take advantage of every high-percentage shot or area in the game. Using this offense, our team rarely falls so far behind that the situation gets desperate. Our 1961-62 team lost two games early in the season by a total of three points; in our 29 victories we averaged more than 17 points per game better than our opponents. The most points scored against us during that season occurred in our Holiday Tournament game at Madison Square Garden against the University of Wisconsin. The Badgers got 71. But the pattern offense described in this book earned 101 points for us in that same game.

Let me add, in conclusion, that a pattern offense such as I have described in these pages *will not work against a zone defense*. Consequently, many teams that we face during a season will throw a zone defense against us, hoping to force us to shoot from the low-percentage areas outside. In chapter 13 I will present the Cincinnati method of penetrating a zone, and I will explore the means by which we make these opponents come out of their zone and play the game we want them to play.

In practice we break our drills down into two types, general and specific, even though there is some overlapping of purpose between the two. Our general drills are designed to teach the fundamentals that are required of all basketball players; our specific drills concentrate on the special skills that are needed to meet specific game situations. In both cases we strive to condition our players in such a manner that their reactions become automatic. During a game a player has little time to think over each situation that arises; he must respond swiftly, with reflexes trained by long, hard hours in practice drills.

Every drill described in this chapter and the next is used in Cincinnati practice sessions over a season. None is designed for show. It is only by drilling faithfully and earnestly on each phase of offense and defense that players are able to put a planned basketball system into effect. The success of the University of Cincinnati system has been built on the drills you will find here.

Scooting Drill, with Mass Movement

Instructions:
1. Players (X) take a defensive stance.
2. Commands are given by leader (O).
3. On command, "Advance," players scoot forward
4. On command, "Retreat," players scoot backwards.
5. On command, "Right," players slide right, with right hand down.

9

GENERAL DRILLS

6. On command, "Left," players slide left, with left hand down.

Purpose: To teach defensive movements for man-to-man guarding. To drill on slide step.

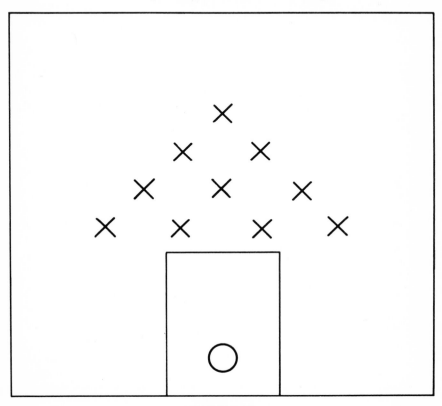

DIAGRAM 38

Three-on-Three, Full Court

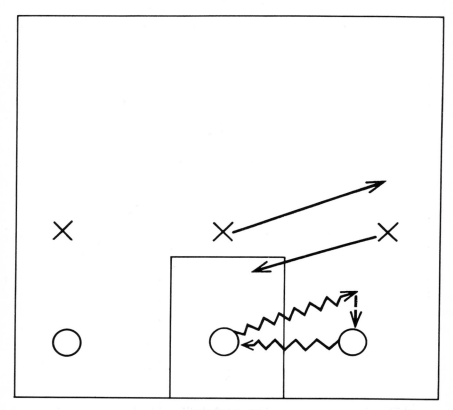

DIAGRAM 39

Instructions: 1. Offense (O) advances up court, moving ball laterally causing defense (X) to switch, slide, or stay.

Purpose: Teaches both offense and defense. In early practices we allow no switching, thus teaching defensive men to slide through.

Truck and Trailer

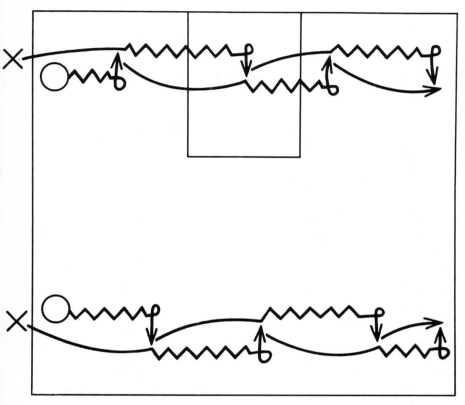

DIAGRAM 40

Instructions: 1. Teams of two men each are used.
2. First man with ball (O) begins in kneeling position. On command he dribbles six to eight yards, trailed by (X). (O) pivots and hands off to (X), who times his movement to be in position for handoff. (O) drags free hand on floor after handoff, then times his speed to take handoff as (X) pivots. This dribble, pivot, and handoff continues across court and back.

Purpose: Teaches offensive movements, especially timing of man cutting off man with ball.

Up and Back, Two-Handed Chest Pass

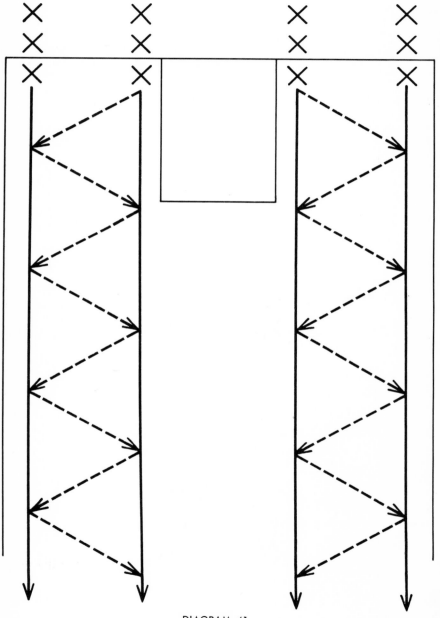

DIAGRAM 41

GENERAL DRILLS

Instructions: 1. Form four lines at end of floor, as shown, one ball to two lines.
2. Pair of men in each double line run full length of court and return, passing ball between them, using two-handed chest pass only.

Purpose: Teaches ball handling while running at top speed. Helps break dribble habit.

Bull in the Ring

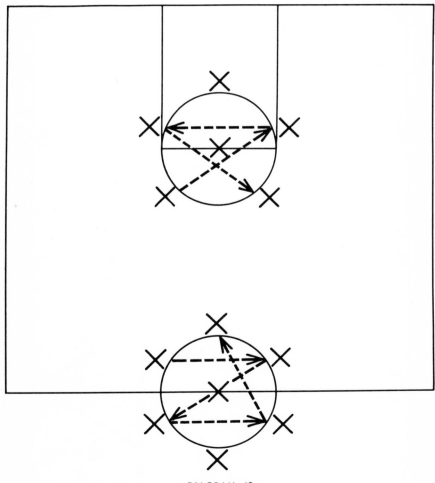

DIAGRAM 42

GENERAL DRILLS

Instructions: 1. At least five men on the circle, with "bull" in the center. Men on circle use various passes to each other, while "bull" tries for interception.
2. Pass cannot be made to man on either side of passer. Lob pass cannot be used.
3. Pass must be made within a three-second count, with "bull" doing the counting.
4. Upon interception, "bull" takes place of last passer.

Purpose: To teach both passing and defense on man with the ball.

Five-on-One Passing

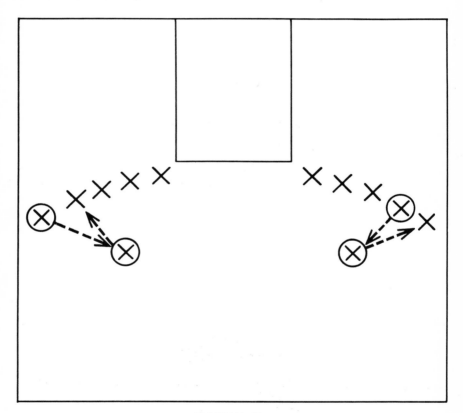

DIAGRAM 43

Instructions: 1. Form half circles of five men, with one more man facing each half circle.
2. One ball begins in half circle, and one ball is held by the man at the center.

3. Two-handed chest passes are made simultaneously. These passes continue, until coach makes change of "out" man.

Purpose: To teach passing and sharpen reflexes.

Two Ball Drill

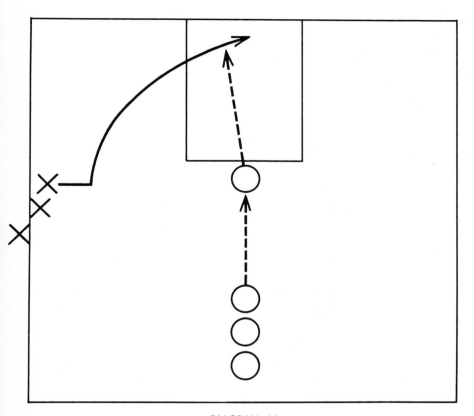

DIAGRAM 44

Instructions: 1. Two lines of players are used, (O) in middle, (X) on side.
2. First (X) fakes, then drives toward basket for pass and lay-up.
3. First (O) fakes, passes in, and follows.
4. Second ball put in play as first pair clears.
5. Follow man (O) retrieves ball after shot and tosses out to (O) line.

6. Lines should be alternated, and both sides of floor should be used.

Purpose: To teach offensive drive and feed pass.

Three Man Weave

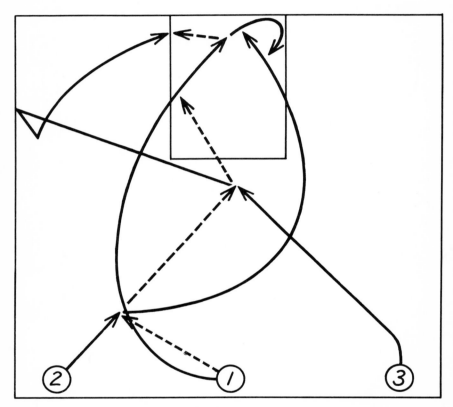

DIAGRAM 45

Instructions:
1. Three men line up at center line.
2. Ball starts in middle position, with No. 1 passing to No. 2, then going behind and around No. 2. No. 2 passes to No. 3, then goes behind and around No. 3.
3. Man who makes last pass goes to side of court, stops, fakes, drives to basket, and takes handoff for the lay-up.
4. Other two men also take shots before drill is complete.

GENERAL DRILLS

5. A reverse pivot may be added before taking the shot.

Purpose: To teach ball handling and timing on full-speed offensive attack.

Five Man Weave

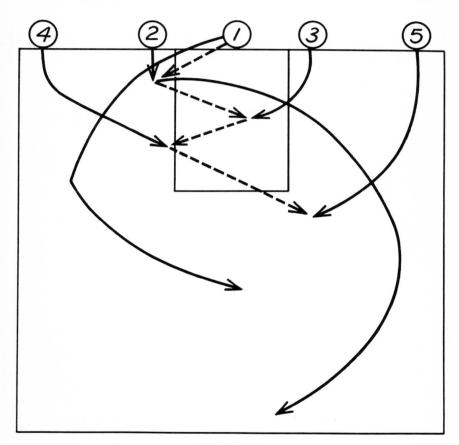

DIAGRAM 46

Instructions: 1. Five men are lined up on endline, with ball in middle position.

                2. No. 1 passes to No. 2, then goes behind and outside *two* men, Nos. 2 and 4. No. 2 then passes to No. 3 and goes behind and outside both No. 3 and No. 5. The pattern remains the same as the ball is moved the full length of the court. Passer

always goes behind and outside two men before returning to middle for a pass. No shots are taken.

Purpose: To teach ball handling and timing on full-speed offensive attack.

Four Corner Passing and Pivoting Drill

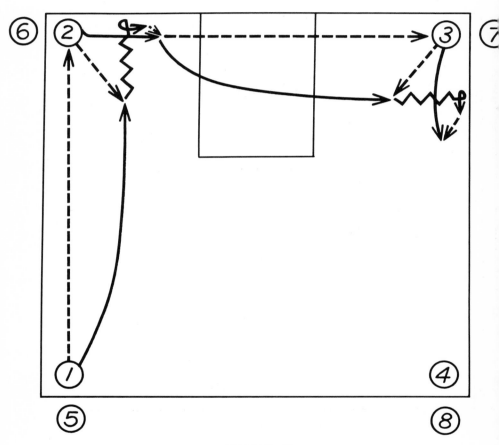

DIAGRAM 47

Instructions: 1. Form lines of players in each of the four corners of a half court. Drill may be run with one ball, two balls diagonally, or one ball in each corner.
2. No. 1 passes to No. 2 and runs at full speed toward the corner. No. 1 gets a return pass from

100

No. 2 about halfway, and continues to the corner, using a dribble, if necessary.

3. At corner, No. 1 pivots and hands off to No. 2, who immediately passes to No. 3, and then follows to the corner, taking a return pass, etc.

4. Drill continues from corner to corner at full speed.

Purpose: To teach offensive movements and good, lead passing.

Two Man Tipping

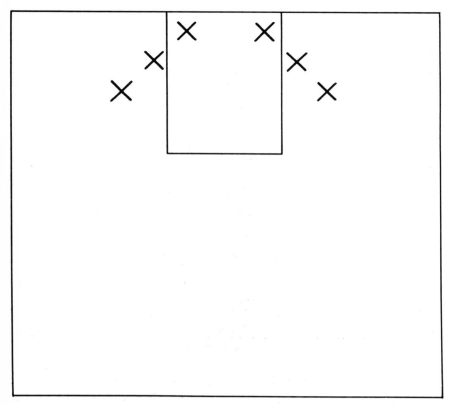

DIAGRAM 48

Instructions: 1. Two men are stationed under the basket.

2. First man tips ball against the board at least three times, then tips it into basket.

3. Second man does same from other side.

101

4. Right hand used on right side, left hand on left side.

Purpose: To teach fingertip control on offensive tips. Man tipping should practice as if he were "squeezing a lemon" with fingertips.

Team Tipping

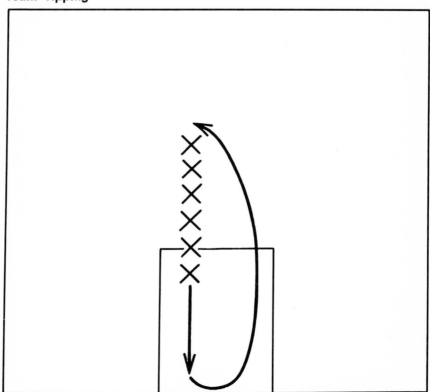

DIAGRAM 49

Instructions: 1. Form a full team line, one behind the other, facing the basket, with the first man in control of the ball.
2. Front man begins the drill by placing the ball high and soft on the boards, to the side of the basket.
3. Next man in line tips the ball high and soft on the board, with fingertip control.
4. Third man continues as preceding man.

5. Remaining men follow, each one tipping as man before him. After tip, man goes to end of line.

Purpose: To teach fingertip control of tips.

Summary

Under no circumstances should these drills be half-hearted or half-serious. Coaches must keep "on top" of the action at all times and immediately correct mistakes. No player can be allowed to take it easy during drills, because there never was a player born who could not show some improvement by working harder.

I have seen poor basketball teams loaf through practice drills, turn drill sessions into periods of horseplay, and, consequently, establish the pattern by which they will play in competition. Such teams do not want to win.

The champion Bearcats go through these drills with snap and precision. They strive to improve their timing and execution with each drill session. The desire to win is at no time more evident than it is in our drill sessions. Since we demand maximum effort, we never run any drill long enough for it to become boring. A little every day is always more effective than a lot once a week.

The drills in this chapter were designed to teach specific skills required by our offensive and defensive systems. In observing these drills on the practice floor a coach should not be too hasty to change successful moves to a stereotyped conception of what constitutes a proper form or style of play. For example, it is proper to go after a defensive rebound with both hands, in order to insure safe possession of the ball, yet Tom Thacker, Cincinnati's jumping-jack guard, has amazingly fast hands and is capable of sweeping a ball off the boards one-handed, locking the ball securely between hand and forearm. George Wilson has the ability to trap an ascending ball against the backboard with one hand and then pluck it off with the other. Both of these rebounds are individual skills, and both are successful. I would be foolish to attempt to change them—but equally foolish, let me add, to adopt either method of rebounding as standard for the Cincinnati team. Exceptions to the rule cannot be taught, but when they are successfully demonstrated by a player and prove more successful for him than the accepted form, let him use them. The one-handed jump shot, the overhand foul shot, and the hook shot were all once exceptions to the rule, remember.

Five-on-Five Rebounding and Fast-Break Drill

Instructions: 1. Coach starts this drill by handling the ball.

SPECIFIC DRILLS

2. Three offensive inside men (O-1, O-1, O-3) move without the ball.
3. The coach either takes a shot or passes to an offensive player who then takes a shot.

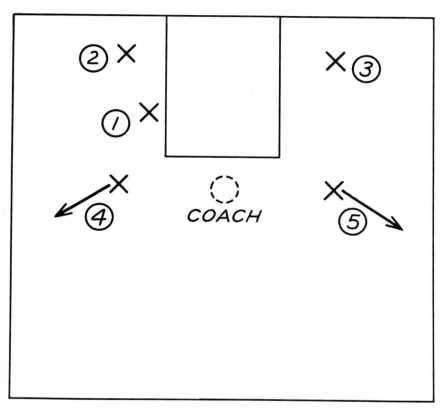

DIAGRAM 50

4. Defensive players (X) are in guarding positions, but allow shot to be made. Defensive players then box-out, while offensive players use head and shoulder fakes and roll-offs to get inside.
5. Defensive guards check their men, then move to the points for pitchout, while offensive guards either try to prevent outlet pass, or move downcourt for defense against the break.
6. Inside offensive men fight for offensive rebound, but do not go downcourt if they lose the rebound.
7. If defense rebounds and pitches out, this becomes

a three-on-two fast break, with the offside rebounder joining the attack.

8. Play this as a game, with an offensive tip-in counting two points, and a fast-break basket counting one point.

Purpose: We use this drill primarily to practice boxing-out on rebounds. Its other values should be self-evident.

One-on-One, with Offensive Pivot

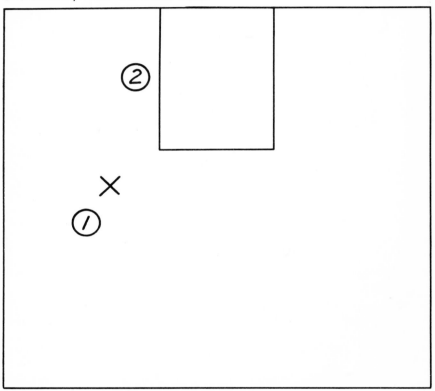

DIAGRAM 51

Instructions: 1. Defensive man (X) plays man-to-man on (O-1). (O-2) can be used as a post for a drive, or (O-1) can feed (O-2) and cut off him.

2. Defensive man must fight over (O-2).

Purpose: To teach man-to-man defense against drive off pivot-screen.

Two-on-Two, Guard-Forward Series, with Offensive Pivot

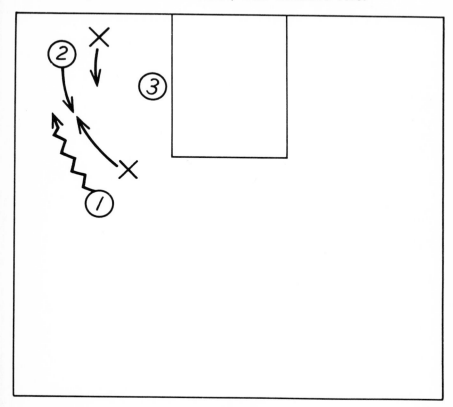

DIAGRAM 52

Instructions: 1. Defensive men (X) must guard offensive men (O-1 and O-2) as they move outside.
2. Defensive men should slide through. As a last resort, they may switch.
3. Offensive men drive off the post at any time and try to score.

Purpose: To teach guard and forward man-to-man defense without switching. Teaches defensive men to fight over pivot-screen. Offensively, we use this drill to teach a guard-forward scissors.

SPECIFIC DRILLS

Two-on-Two, Guard Series, with Offensive Post

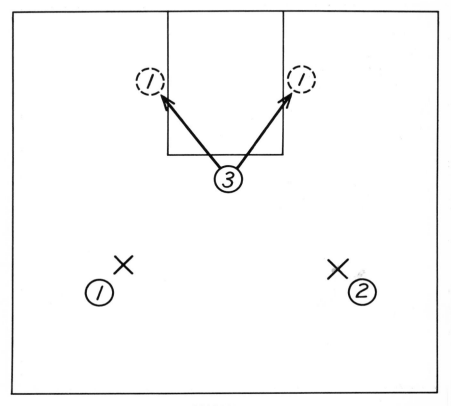

DIAGRAM 53

Instructions: 1. Pivot man plays high or low post.
                   2. Offensive guards (O-1 and O-2) use their various offensive maneuvers to score.

Purpose: Man-to-man defense of offensive guards. Offensive value is self-evident.

Two Pass Pivot Drill

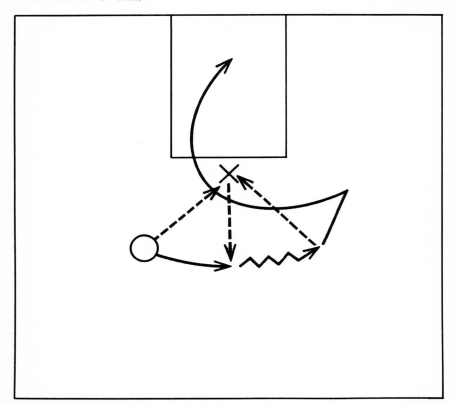

DIAGRAM 54

Instructions: 1. Offensive guard passes to pivot man and moves right for return pass.
2. Guard dribbles right and passes back to pivot man.
3. Guard cuts off pivot man and takes handoff, or pivot man fakes handoff and shoots.
4. Can be run in opposite direction.

Purpose: To teach hard passes to pivot. To teach timing on cut off the pivot.

Cut-Throat 21

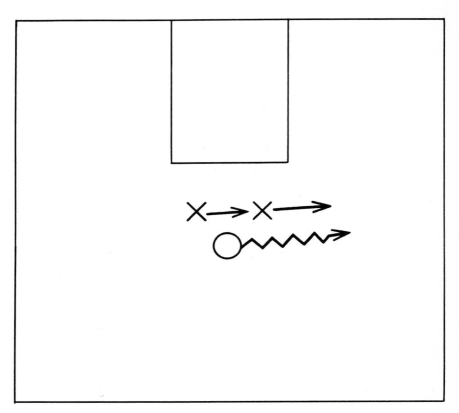

DIAGRAM 55

Instructions: 1. One offensive man is matched against two defensive men.
2. Game starts with offensive man (O) in possession
of ball.
3. When (O) gets shot off, all three men scramble
for the rebound.
4. If (O) shoots field goal, he shoots free throws.
On missed free throw all three men scramble for
the ball.
5. If shooter makes three free throws in a row, he
starts at original offensive position.
6. Man who recovers a missed shot becomes offensive
man.

SPECIFIC DRILLS

7. Count two points for field goal and one point for foul shot. First man to reach 21 points wins.

Purpose: To teach shooting under pressure, and to encourage aggressiveness.

One-on-One Plus Offensive Trailer

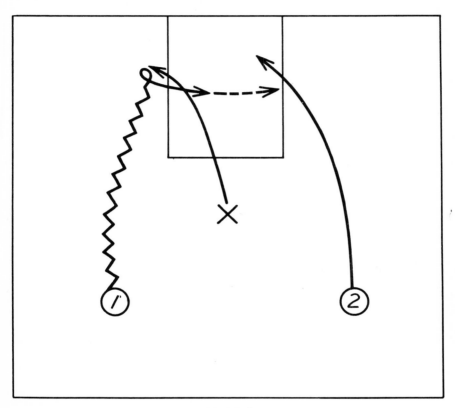

DIAGRAM 56

Instructions: 1. Offensive man (O-1) drives downcourt.
2. When defensed by (X), (O-1) stops, pivots and passes to trailer (O-2).
3. If (X) falls off, (O-1) may take a shot.

Purpose: To teach two-on-one fast-break attack. Also teaches reverse pivot.

Two-on-One Plus Defensive Trailer

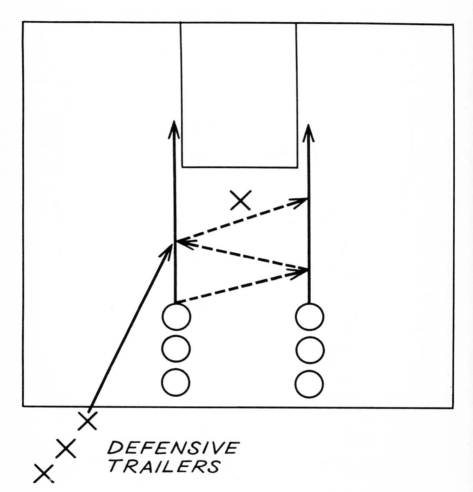

DIAGRAM 57

Instructions: 1. Two offensive men (O) pass back and forth trying to make defensive man (X) at middle commit
to one side or other.
2. Offensive men start on command, "Go."
3. Defensive trailer starts on count of two after command to go.

Purpose: To teach continuous effort by defensive trailer
against fast break.

Three-on-Two Plus Defensive Trailer

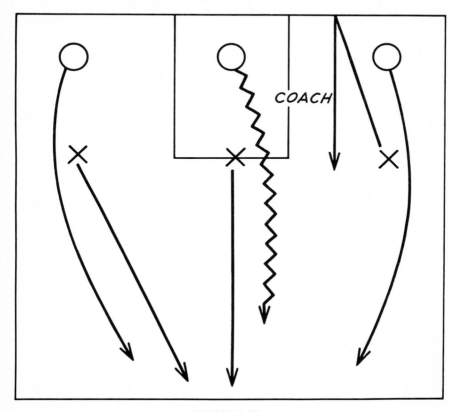

DIAGRAM 58

Instructions: 1. Offensive players are (O).
2. Defensive players are (X).
3. Coach calls out the name of a defensive player. This player must run back behind offensive players and touch baseline.
4. As coach calls name of man who will be defensive trailer, he tosses ball to offensive man. Offense breaks downcourt in a three-on-two fast break.
5. Defensive pair should take tandem positions. Top man challenges the ball, and the back man guards the first pass in the offensive triangle. Top man then drops back to force shot from outside.
6. Trailer tries to get in on the play.

Purpose: To teach defense against the fast break.

Continuous Fast Break, with Eleven Men

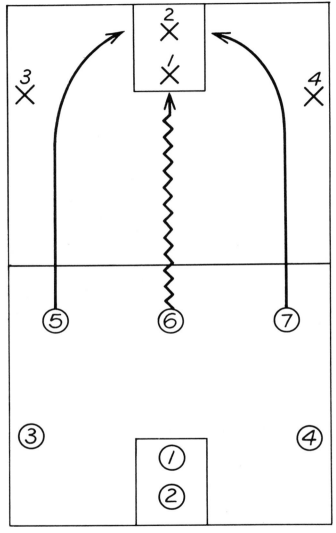

DIAGRAM 59

Instructions: 1. Use eleven men as shown in *Diagram 59*.
2. Three men (O-5, O-6, and O-7) take the ball down the floor on a fast break.
3. (X¹) and (X²) defense the break from tandem

positions. Top man challenges the ball, back man takes the first pass, and top man drops off to side opposite the pass.

4. When the shot is made, all five men become rebounders. Whoever gets the rebound pitches out to the side to (X^3) or (X^4), who both then move to the center.

5. The rebounder fills the center lane for the fast break in the opposite direction.

6. The four remaining men, of the five who were rebounding, fill in the four positions, two in tandem in the foul lane, and two as outlet men on the sides.

7. This drill continues without a break until the coach is satisfied with the offense, defense, ball handling, rebounding, passing, and floor positions.

Purpose: The fast break, and defense against it.

ILLUSTRATION X

The "red shirts" in a moment of triumph.

Summary

In these two chapters on drills I have described the foundation upon which our basketball system is built. The habits developed by drilling are applied in every situation that arises in a ball game. At the high school level the fundamentals of dribbling, passing, shooting, and individual guarding must become automatic. At the college level we rely upon these basic skills, of course, but we attempt to make sliding through, going tandem, rolling on a switch, boxing-out, and cutting off a pivot screen just as automatic. It takes constant practice to perform these functions without conscious thought. There is no other road to winning basketball.

In our Swing-and-Go series, detailed in chapter 6, the forward who acts as swing-man must develop the habit of facing the basket immediately after he receives the pass, without using his dribble. On this one move depends the success of the key play in the key series of our entire offense. As this book goes to press our forwards are drilling on this move in a simple little In-and-Out Drill, taking a pass and facing the basket, taking a pass and facing the basket, taking the pass and facing the basket—each time trying to make the movement automatic, a reflex, a part of themselves. If they had time, they could look up and see the banners, hanging at each end of the University of Cincinnati Fieldhouse, and proclaiming:

NCAA CHAMPIONS 1961

NCAA CHAMPIONS 1962

These are invitations to practice harder.

Although many coaches might argue that almost every move in basketball involves a special situation, we use this term to refer to those aspects of the game which involve the entire team but are still separate from the normal offensive-defensive action on the court. Such situations arise on a jump-ball, on an out-of-bounds play, and on a freeze. Each requires special planning, special practice, and special application during a game. Over the course of a season each of these situations will arise enough times, and affect the results of enough ball games, to make all of this special attention worth while.

The Jump-Ball

My assistant coach, Tay Baker, and I once started out to list all possible jump-ball situations, with the object of teaching them to our players. When we reached 92 separate and distinct possibilities, we quit. No player can be expected to learn such a great mass of material and apply it during a ball game. Instead, a coach must boil down as many situations as he can imagine into a few general factors, and from these factors formulate general rules for his players to follow. Our rules and their application, as described in this chapter, will not cover every possibility, but they have been very successful for us.

SPECIAL SITUATIONS

SPECIAL SITUATIONS

General Rules on All Jump-Balls

RULE 1. Always maintain an "open spot" for the tip. (An open spot is that place on the circle where two of your men are together, with no opposing player between them.)

RULE 2. Always play for possession when you have the advantage. (That is, when you have the better jumper.)

RULE 3. On even jumps, crash defensively.

RULE 4. On disadvantage situations (other team has better jumper) assume defensive positions, but gamble one man on a crash.

RULE 5. Always keep four men on the circle.

In addition to these rules, we instruct our players to match the opposing pattern on the circle. If they are in a box, we also get into a box; if they are in a diamond, we form a diamond.

The Center-Court Jump-Ball. On jumps in the center circle, we are interested in possession only, therefore you will find no plays designed to follow the situations diagrammed. On those occasions when a clear opening to the basket presents itself, our players will free lance in an attempt to score, but in most situations we go into our regular pattern offense once possession of the ball is assured.

In *Diagram 60* I show the two most popular alignments used on jump-ball situations. If the circles (O) represent our team and the x-marks (X) represent the opposition, it can be seen that in either the Box or the Diamond we have two men together, forming an "open

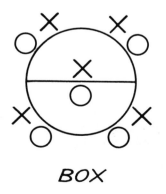
BOX

DIAMOND

DIAGRAM 60

Most common formations used on jump-ball situations are the box and the diamond. Both give each team an "open spot."

spot." The opposition also will have two men together, and it is here that we will crash when the necessity arises.

It is the responsibility of the tipper to check the location of our open spot before the jump. Our four men on the circle try to establish this spot for the convenience of the tipper. Whether he is left-handed or right-handed, for example, will determine how this open spot is established. The position of the official tossing the ball must also be taken into account. When we have the advantage on the center-court jump, the ball will be tipped to the open spot. The men on either side of this spot must prevent a crash and then gain possession of the ball.

Diagram 61 illustrates an even jump at center court, with both teams in box formation. In this situation we crash the obvious man into the opposition's open spot. (The obvious man is a player selected by the coach for one of many reasons, including deception, ability to handle his opponent, or speed.) Our tip, in the case illustrated, would be back to our open spot.

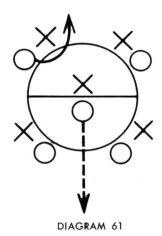

DIAGRAM 61

An even jump at center court. Cincinnati represented by (O).

On a center-court jump, with our team at a disadvantage, we take defensive positions, making certain that the opposition's open spot is away from their offensive basket. Having encouraged them to tip back, we crash our obvious man into this spot.

The Offensive Court Jump-Ball. With the advantage, or with an even jump in our offensive court, our first concern is to prevent a crash into our open spot. Since our opponents will line up in defensive positions, this open spot will be away from our offensive basket. On these jumps, as on the center-court jumps, we strive for possession rather than for a quick, "fancy-Dan" basket. *Diagram 62* shows a normal situation on the offensive-court circle, with the advantage ours. Notice that our upcourt men box first, and then go for the ball.

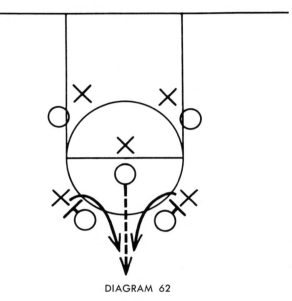

DIAGRAM 62

An offensive-court jump. Cincinnati with the advantage.

On an even jump in the offensive court our two men nearest the basket are instructed to jockey back and forth to cover the sides. Since a tip by the opposition *toward our offensive basket* is less likely than a tip to the side, a bit more pressure can be exerted toward the side. Our own tip, if we get it, will be back to the open spot, as usual, with our upcourt men boxing-out first, and then gaining possession of the ball.

When we are at a disadvantage we assume defensive positions and chance a crash by the obvious man into our opponent's open spot. Since the opposition must take the ball the length of the court if they gain possession, we take a chance on crashing and then recovering quickly into our defensive man-to-man.

The Defensive Court Jump-Ball. In our defensive court we do not hesitate to tip back when we have the advantage. Our object is still gaining possession of the ball, and we view a tip here in much the same way we view a defensive rebound. If we box-out before going for the ball, the percentages are with us. Far too may coaches hesitate to instruct their players to take advantage of the basket-side open spot when they are in their defensive court, but we have found this a satisfactory way to get the ball. Our advantage here is increased because the opponents on our basket-side men will not play tight—until they read this.

Diagram 63 illustrates a diamond formation set up for an even jump in our defensive court. In this situation we move a second man on the opponent nearest the basket and crash into our opponent's open spot. The tip, if we get it, goes to our open spot.

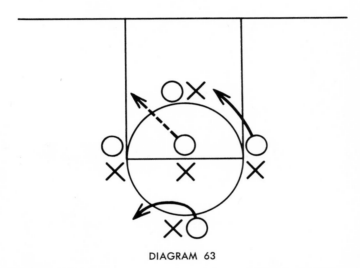

DIAGRAM 63

A defensive-court jump. Jumpers are even. One defensive player cheats toward most dangerous man. Second defensive player crashes into opponent's open shot.

When the jump in our defensive court is even we endeavor to tip to our tallest, best jumping man, making certain that he is one of the men forming our open spot.

If we are at a disadvantage in our defensive court, we are in trouble. In this case we assume defensive positions again, but overplay on the basket-side, hoping to force the tip back. Against both box and diamond we will crash the most obvious man.

Whenever possible, in a diamond formation, we try to force the opposition's open spot on the same side as the official tossing up the ball, or on the side least convenient to the opposition's jumper.

ILLUSTRATION XI

Tipping to the "open spot." Cincinnati players, Bonham and Thacker, in the foreground are boxing-out their men, keeping the spot open for the tip.

SPECIAL SITUATIONS

Out-of-Bounds Plays

Our object in bringing the ball in from our defensive endline, or from the side, is merely to put the ball in play. If our opponents apply pressure on our receiver, we screen the man pressured in order to free him to receive the pass. Under our offensive basket, however, we use several set plays which are designed to score quick baskets.

In general, the following suggestions should be followed when planning out-of-bounds plays:

1. Keep them simple.
2. Take advantage of your best passer, screener, and shooter.
3. Always be ready to counter with at least one option play.
4. Have your rebound strength near the basket when the shot is taken.
5. Keep your opponents guessing at all times. Use one formation, or formations that seem the same, then change plays with timed signals.

Foul Line Play. This play is designed for the best outside shooter on the team. The four men inbounds line up along the foul line, with the man who is to take the shot at the far left as they face the basket. The next two men in line should be big and strong, for their job is to prevent the defensive men from breaking through. On the extreme right should be your playmaker. The play breaks as illustrated in *Diagram 64.* The out-of-bounds man, who should be your best passer, starts action with a signal, slapping the ball or dropping an upraised hand.

Since this is one of our standard plays, I have designated the offense with the numbers of our players who ran it in the 1962 NCAA Tournament. Wilson (32) slaps the ball to key the play, and Yates (20) breaks suddenly to the side to receive the ball. Hogue (22) and Thacker (25) set up a shoulder-to-shoulder screen. Bonham (21) waits until Yates receives the ball, then fakes toward the basket and cuts behind the screen to take a pass from Yates and get off a jump shot.

Options on this play are determined by the defense. In many cases the defense can be trapped into making a mistake, if you run this version several times. Once they are convinced this is the only option, they may leave themselves vulnerable to a breakthrough down the middle. The play can be run from either side, of course.

Cut-Off Play. On this play we station three men on the foul line and one at a low-post position on the ball side. *Diagrams 65 and 66*

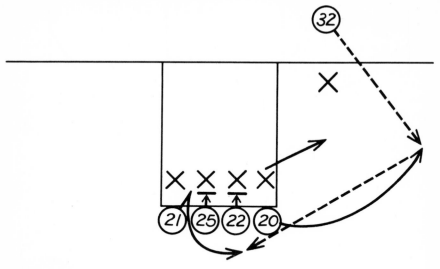

DIAGRAM 64

Foul Line Play. No. 20 breaks outside for pass inbounds. No. 21 fakes and then cuts behind double screen set up by Nos. 25 and 22. No. 20 passes to No. 21 for the shot.

illustrate the two options we use. In *Diagram 65* Thacker (25) tries to free himself by setting up his man to the inside and then breaking outside to receive the ball. From here he can shoot or feed Hogue (22). After running this option several times, we change to the option shown in *Diagram 66.* Again Thacker breaks toward Hogue, but this time he fakes going outside, then quickly reverses direction and cuts inside to take the pass and lay it up. No matter which of the two options is used, the man on the right of the foul line goes in to rebound, and the man in the middle drops back as a safety man.

In spite of their extreme simplicity—or maybe because of it—these plays have proved very effective for us in major collegiate competition.

Triple Threat Play. Less simple, but equally effective, is the out-of-bounds play I have shown in *Diagram 67.* Opponents often confuse this formation with that of the Cut-Off Play, although the men on the foul line are much closer together for screening purposes. This time the man on the low post is the key man, and he has three options, his choice depending upon the defense. (Since it is late in the game, I am going to put in a new team for this one.)

Heidotting (24), playing the low-post position, can break to the

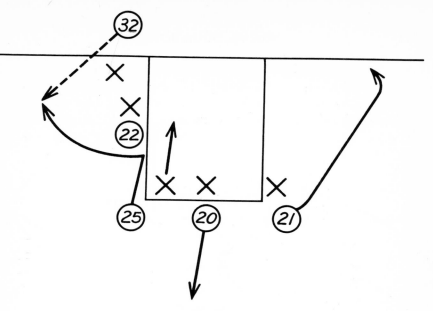

DIAGRAM 65

Cut-Off Play. No. 25 sets up his defensive man to the inside, then cuts off No. 22 and goes outside for the pass.

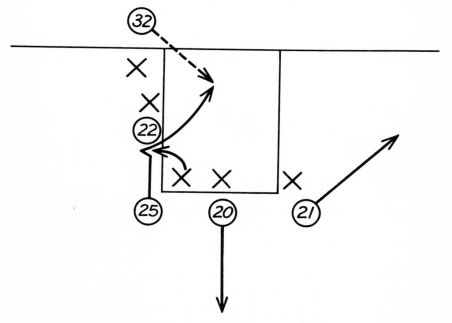

DIAGRAM 66

Cut-Off Play Inside. No. 25 sets up his man with a fake to the outside, then cuts off No. 22 to go inside for the pass.

basket for a quick pass and lay-up. If his man overplays to the inside to prevent such a move, Heidotting can break outside and take the pass there. From this position he has two options: he can feed a return pass to Dierking (15) and screen for him, or he can pass out to Shingleton (11) who has cut behind the shoulder-to-shoulder screen on the foul line.

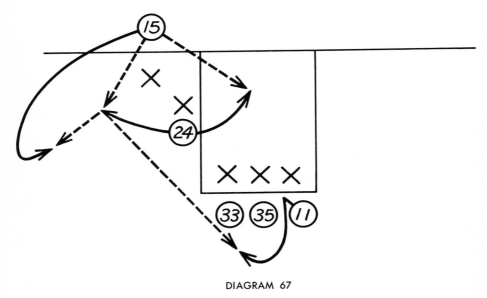

DIAGRAM 67

Triple Threat Play. No. 24 may move inside or outside. If he moves outside for the inbounds pass, he can hit No. 24 or hit No. 11 behind the screen on the foul line.

The Freeze

Freezing the ball late in a game to protect a lead is not only ethical but is also "good basketball." Freezing the ball early in a game merely to hold down your opponent's score is questionable on both counts. Not too many years ago basketball fans were treated to the spectacle of so-called "slowdown basketball." Underdog teams would gain possession of the ball and literally sit on it for long periods of time in an effort to keep the opposition from scoring. In an effort to return the game to its original spirit, rulesmakers instituted the five-second rule, which forces the man with the ball to pass or dribble within five seconds after gaining possession, *if defensive pressure is put on him.* Incidents in which offensive teams hold the ball in order to force a defensive team out of a

126

rigid zone defense still occur, but this type of freezing does nothing to help the game of basketball.

Our Cincinnati teams have gained a reputation over the past few years as deliberate, ball-controlling, defense-minded basketball squads. *But we have never played a stalling game, except to protect a lead late in the second half.* At such times, when freezing is the best strategy, we use what I consider to be one of the most effective freezes in basketball today, and I claim no credit for its creation. Hank Iba's great Oklahoma State teams used this particular freeze against our Cincinnati teams with such outstanding success several years ago that we just naturally adopted it for our own use. Out of respect for its origin we still call it the Oklahoma State Freeze in our own practices.

The Oklahoma State Freeze. The moves and the passing involved in this freeze are designed with a dual purpose, either to eat up time or to score. If time is the important factor, we do not shoot out of this pattern, no matter how attractive the opportunity. *Diagram 68* illustrates the movements of the offensive team using the Oklahoma State Freeze. The Pivot Man (22) plays on the foul line, acting as safety man as the freeze begins. He keeps on the move at all times, faking toward the basket and then breaking out to his left or right as shown. Since his

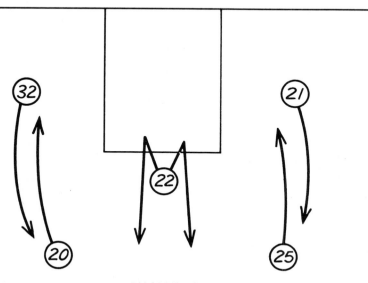

DIAGRAM 68

The Oklahoma State Freeze. No. 22 moves toward basket and out constantly, while guards and forwards keep exchanging positions.

defensive man must play behind him to protect the basket, the Pivot Man should be free to catch the ball as he comes out toward midcourt. If his defensive man gets desperate and plays him to the side, the Pivot Man can be fed from the side. He then has an easy chance to roll to the basket.

Forwards and guards on each side exchange positions constantly, watching for an early switch that will allow a break to the basket. All five men must move at the same time, staying in the same alignment. Crossing at midcourt must be avoided. Passing is done from outside to outside, or outside to pivot, until a man breaks clear under the basket.

Keep-Away. If the defense begins pressing in an attempt to trap or double-team the man with the ball, we change to a keep-away tactic, placing three men out and two men in. The players using this type of freeze are trained to "pass and cut away." When a pass is made, the passer quickly goes opposite the ball and, if possible, cuts for the basket. The offense then rotates into the vacated spot, as illustrated in *Diagram 69.* By passing and going away, the offense should be able to prevent double-teaming while keeping potential scoring pressure on the defense.

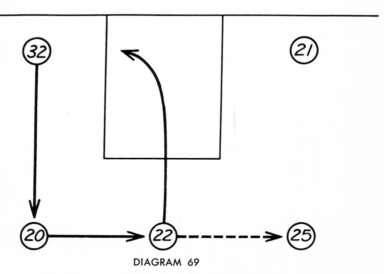

DIAGRAM 69

Keep Away. Player who passes always cuts away. Other players rotate to fill his position.

Good passing is essential during a freeze. Ball handling must be sure, and every player must remain calm in the face of the opposition's mounting desperation to get the ball. Mistakes at this time can cost a ball game.

Many modern basketball teams employ the press as part of their regular defense, using it at intervals throughout a ball game. Other teams utilize it only late in the game, when they are trailing, or when possession of the ball is vital. Cincinnati, as I stated in chapter 3, is one of the latter, even though we practice the full-court press from the start of the season in order to develop man-to-man defensive skills. We are not unfamiliar with presses during games, however, because we have faced them in most of our games. In this chapter I want to describe the methods we use to combat both the full-court press and the half-court press. Since the man-to-man press is so much a part of our own practice sessions, we have no specific assignments worked out to beat it. We may have to screen the receiver to free him for the inbounds pass, but after that he is on his own, as long as he faces a one-on-one situation.

To make certain that a trap (double-team) does not develop, our guard without the ball has the responsibility of keeping his man with him and away from the guard with the ball. Should the defensive man on the guard without the ball try to set up a trap, this guard should make certain he is in position for a pass. He does this *by remaining on line with the ball as he comes up the floor*. Failure to do this is an invitation to the opposition to trap the man with the ball.

12 COMBATING THE PRESS

COMBATING THE PRESS

The 3-1-1 Zone Press

The most common full-court press used against Cincinnati is the 3-1-1. *Diagram 70* illustrates the mechanics of this particular defensive maneuver. As our guards prepare to bring the ball inbounds our opponents throw three men, Nos. 4, 5, and 3 across our defensive forecourt. Defensive man No. 2 occupies the center of the floor, and No. 1 drops back as deep zone man. The idea here is for Nos. 4 and 5 to trap the receiver, G, when we bring the ball in play.

Against this press, our Pivot Man immediately goes deep to our offensive baseline, forcing No. 1 to cover him. Our forwards, F and f, go to midcourt and spread wide. Our inbounds pass goes to G, and Nos. 4 and 5 defensive men move in quickly to trap him. At the same time No. 2 must move to cover the forward on the ball side, F. As soon as he passes in the ball, our out-of-bounds man moves out on line with the receiver, as shown, forcing No. 3 to cover two men, g and f.

Our second pass is determined by No. 3's coverage. If he covers g, the pass is made to f, as illustrated. If No. 3 covers f, then the pass goes to g.

Now that we have the ball in play, what do we do with it? Study *Diagram 70* carefully; it contains elements that often make a full-court press backfire. If the second pass can be made to f, for example, we have a three-on-two situation from midcourt to our offensive basket, and we play for a quick score.

Occasionally, we pass directly to one of the spread forwards from out-of-bounds, creating a quick three-on-two.

Should the second pass be made to g, he can take the ball upcourt on a dribble, getting help from the forward on his side, if he needs it.

Using the same attack, we can also bring the ball upcourt against a 2-1-2 zone press.

The purpose of any full-court press is to pressure the offensive team into a turnover. Inexperienced teams facing a press will allow themselves to be trapped, fail to move the ball across the ten-second line, or be forced into a bad pass. Experienced teams try to use the defensive trap as a weapon against the defensive team. Whenever a trap takes place, *one offensive man is free*. This man is the key man when it comes to defeating the full-court press, and it is this man who can convert what looks like a desperate situation for the offense into a sudden three-on-two, or three-on-one sweep to the basket.

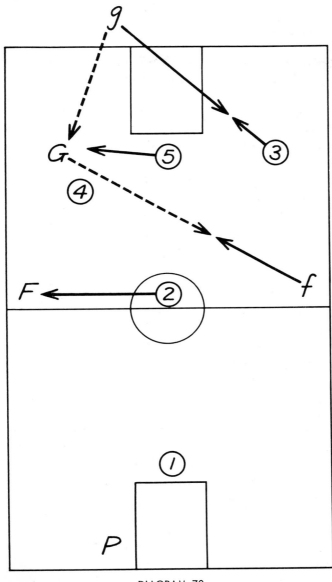

DIAGRAM 70

Attacking the 3-1-1 Zone Press. As No. 2 covers the forward on the ball side, *f* becomes free to move in for a pass. Note that P has gone all the way to the endline to pull No. 1 out of the action. A pass to *f* gives the offense a three-on-two.

COMBATING THE PRESS

Half-Court Presses

Half-court zone presses have become very popular in modern collegiate basketball. While these formations resemble standard zone defenses, their object is not the same. A standard zone defense is set up in the half-court to protect the basket by protecting the high-percentage areas. The half-court press, on the other hand, is aimed specifically at *getting the ball* by traps or interceptions of passes. In order to apply this kind of pressure, the defensive team must be aligned in such a manner that double-teaming the guard bringing up the ball is possible near the center-line, or double-teaming this guard *and a deep man* is possible after the ball is brought safely across the center-line. In the former case, we find a 1-2-2 most often used against us, and in the latter case, a 1-2-1-1.

The 1-2-2 Half-Court Press. This formation may sometimes be considered a 3-2 alignment, although it is most effective when the middle man is definitely out ahead of the two flanking front men, as illustrated in *Diagram 71.* Being "on the point," he forces the offensive guards to commit the ball to one side of the court or the other before they cross the center-line, predetermining the side where the trap will take place. Our attack against this zone can be followed in *Diagram 71.* We bring an agile, good ball-handling man into the high-post position and send two men deep, one on each side of the foul lane. As our guards bring the ball across the center-line, maintaining their usual line-of-ball positions (neither man ahead of the other), we will assume they are forced to commit to the left, as illustrated. Defensive man No. 3 moves forward to prevent a pass to g, the guard without the ball. No. 4 and No. 5 close on the man with the ball, G, in an attempt to trap him. As soon as the defense makes its move, our deep man on the left of the foul lane breaks out to a wide position on the extended foul line, and our deep man on the opposite side of the lane moves across to the ball side, remaining deep.

Having made the moves shown in *Diagram 71,* we are now in position to turn this press against itself. If defensive man No. 2 follows F, then No. 1 is given the problem of guarding both f and P. The passes from the guard being trapped are shown in *Diagram 72.* He may hit the high-post man directly, or he may pass in to F, who then can hit the high-post man. There have been times, also, when our guard was able

132

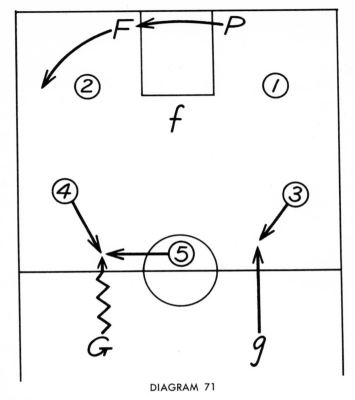

DIAGRAM 71

Attacking the 1-2-2 Half-Court Press. f goes to the foul line while the deep men overload the ball side.

to pass all the way in to P, which is a good way to discourage this type of defense.

The best option against the 1-2-2, as far as the initial pass is concerned, will be dictated by the movements of the defensive men. Practice against this half-court press will soon reveal the defensive possibilities and enable a coach to devise options to counter them. Right here a word seems in order concerning practice against special types of defense or offense. A team cannot possibly learn, and keep in mind, every maneuver against every system of play used in basketball. This is where the scouting report is vital. Your practice against a 1-2-2 should take place when the scouting report reveals that your next opponent is known to use it. Seldom will a team adopt a new system of play from one game to another, so you can be reasonably certain of what offense and defense you will have to face in any particular game. Our own Cincinnati system has remained

133

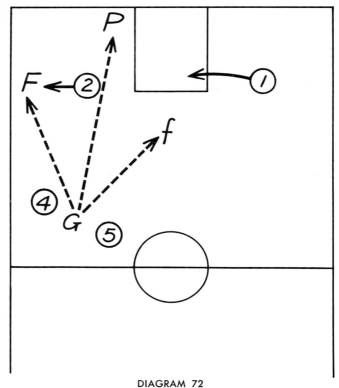

DIAGRAM 72

Attacking the 1-2-2 Half-Court Press. The overload gives G three pass options, depending on the defensive coverage.

basically unchanged since we instituted it in 1960. We reserve the right to throw in a few surprises on any given night, but we make no major changes for any game.

The 1-2-1-1 Half-Court Press. As an example of a press that presents good trapping situations, this one is excellent. Ohio State University perfected the 1-2-1-1 during the past few years, and few teams can match the Buckeyes in making it work. We studied *Diagram 73* closely prior to our games with these same Buckeyes, and spent a good deal of time devising ways to beat such a defense. Actually, as *Diagram 73* clearly reveals, the opportunities for trapping either the guard with the ball or the forward who gets a pass from that guard are outstanding. Should the guard escape the trap by making his pass to the forward, defensive man No. 2 and defensive man No. 3 can double-team the forward quickly. A pass to the man on the high post is also dangerous, since he can be double- or triple-teamed. But our strategy is to get the ball to the Pivot Man, P, at the high post and force the defense into a 1-3-1 by one of the methods we use to attack the 1-3-1 (described in chapter 13).

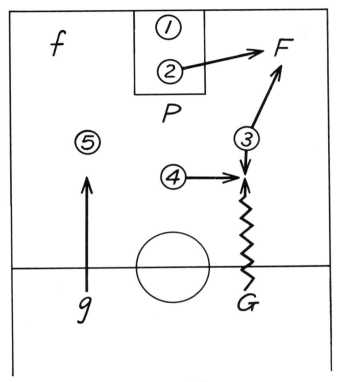

DIAGRAM 73

The Ohio State 1-2-1-1 Half-Court Zone Press. The best attack is a pass to P, which should force the defense into a 1-3-1.

Thorough practice against this press proved a necessity. This was an action situation which developed as the ball was brought past the center-line; it was not a case of a zone being formed and waiting while we were still bringing the ball inbounds. Our attack, to force the 1-3-1 situation, also had to develop quickly as the first trap began to take place. Good, quick passes were essential, and a big, strong man on the high post was a must.

In general the half-court presses lose their effectiveness once the ball is fed to the high-post man, who is at the vertex of a triangle made up of himself and the two deep men. From this triangle most zones can be attacked successfully.

Cincinnati does not use a half-court press of the types described in this chapter. The nature of our normal pressure defense is such (see chapters 3 and 4) that we constantly exert pressure on the man with the ball. We are always ready to trap him, if an offensive mistake invites the trap. With our aggressive, harassing, man-to-man defense, we feel that a planned half-court zone press is unnecessary.

In chapters 6, 7, and 8, I was careful to state that our regular offensive patterns are used against man-to-man defenses. In major collegiate competition the man-to-man defense predominates, and coaches must design their basic offense to combat the type of defense their teams will face most. On the other hand, every basketball coach—especially the high school coach—realizes that his team must be prepared to attack the zone at some time during the season. Cincinnati is no exception, in this respect. Over the course of a full season we can expect to face the zone from time to time. Perhaps, with our reputation as a team that shies away from the long, outside shot, we run into more zone defenses than normal. Whatever the reason, it is necessary for us to have a zone attack as part of our general offensive system. In this chapter I intend to describe the features of our offense that work successfully against zone defenses, and I will make some comments at the end of the chapter concerning *Combination Defenses,* which, in my opinion, are destined to become the predominant college defenses in years to come.

The Theory of the Zone Defense

Standard zone defenses are used for a number of reasons, all of them valid. In high school play, narrow basketball courts make the zone effective because it is possible for players on defense to cover both the danger-

13

ATTACKING THE ZONE DEFENSE

ous area near the basket and the vulnerable corners with a minimum of spreading to the side. Since the purpose of a zone defense is to give a defensive man an assigned area to guard, rather than an assigned man, it is also possible to keep the strongest rebounders in good position to rebound. Fast-breaking teams using the zone can be certain that their outlet men are always in the proper position to get the fast break going.

Defense is easier to play in a zone than it is in man-to-man. Movements follow the movement of the ball rather than the movement of the individually assigned offensive man. Screens, fakes, and free-lancing lose their effectiveness because they operate best against a one-on-one situation. Clear, safe lanes for passing are difficult to open up in a zone defense, and less individual effort is called for to prevent offensive men from getting off or receiving passes. Over-all, the defensive team expends less energy in a zone defense than it would playing man-to-man. Thus, taking all of these factors together, this is a type of defense that has great appeal for high school coaches, since their players have less pre-season practice than collegiate players, lack individual defensive skills, and do not yet possess the stamina required to play an entire game of aggressive man-to-man defense.

Collegiate teams use zone defenses, less for the reason that such defenses are easier to play, than for the reason that such defenses can be used to upset their opponent's regular attack. During a particular game a collegiate team may change from man-to-man to zone and back to man-to-man, varying their defense to break the tempo of the opposition, to force the opposition out of its most successful patterns, or to better match a strong rebounding team.

Viewing the standard zone defense objectively, one is forced to admit that its value is evident in many situations. It has been a part of basketball for a long time, and will remain a part of basketball for a longer time still to come. Although zone defenses are outlawed in professional basketball at the moment, I see no reason to try to eliminate them in collegiate competition. The high scoring, offensive spectacle of the professional contest is designed for the spectator; in high school and college we should be more concerned with team play and coaching strategy, and the zone definitely has a place in both.

At Cincinnati we do not use the zone defense because we feel that its disadvantages far outweigh its advantages as a method of stopping an offensive attack. Among these disadvantages I would include the fact that men cannot be matched according to speed, height, and ability, one of the factors that makes man-to-man competition such a dramatic test of individual against individual. There is also too much dependence on the other man to do the job. Every high school coach has heard the post-game argument by his players over which man was responsible for which points by the opposition, because there was confusion as to the exact limits of the zone being covered. Finally, and probably most important, our teams do not use a zone defense because I feel that such defenses are extremely vulnerable. A disciplined, good passing, aggressive ball team, schooled in the methods of penetrating zone defenses, will face them happily and delight in exploiting their weaknesses. Even the re-bounding advantage that supposedly goes automatically with a zone de-fense can be offset by sending extra men to the boards and stopping the fast break before it begins.

Basic Zone Attacks

In setting up the Cincinnati offense against the standard zone, we generalized our attack as follows:

1. Against any zone with an odd number of men out, we use an even number of men out.
2. Against any zone with an even number of men out, we use an odd number of men out.

In practice against various zone defenses, we assign men to positions according to their own individual abilities. We try to keep our attacks balanced, so that they will be effective either to the left or to the right. As always, we strive for simplicity of offensive patterns and a minimum of passing, while working for the good, close-in, high-percentage shot.

Attack Against the 2-3 Zone. Following our rules for evens-and-odds, we attack the 2-3 Zone as shown in *Diagram 74*. With our Pivot Man at the high post and our forwards wide on the extended foul line, we send a guard through the zone as illustrated, forming a 1-3-1 offen-sive formation. (Note that this puts one guard, an *odd number,* out.) In this diagram, G is assumed to have the ball.

The extended foul line positions of our forwards usually split the positions of the two men on the sides of the zone, making these forwards the responsibility of the outside deep men in the zone.

As a result of sending g deep to the side of the foul lane, we have now gained the advantage of having three men in the zones covered by only two of our opponents. Since our deep guard can move from one side of the lane to the other, this advantage can shuttle from side to side,

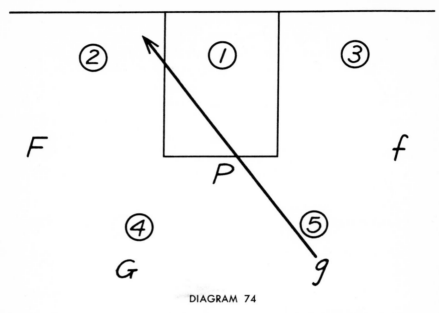

DIAGRAM 74

First step in attacking a 2-3 Zone. Send a guard through the zone.

even though the ball remains in the possession of our outside guard. *Diagram 75* illustrates our advantage to the left, with defensive men Nos. 1 and 2 responsible for our offensive men *P, F,* and *g.*

Once the offense has assumed this 1-3-1 formation, the attack consists of reactions to the defensive moves. We are prepared to counter whatever decisions defensive men Nos. 1 and 2 make, and they *must* decide whom to cover, because we have one man free in their zones. In *Diagram 76* I have illustrated one option available to us after we force No. 1 to cover the deep guard. Here the guard with the ball passes to the Strong Side Forward, *F,* bringing defensive man No. 2 out. *F* then passes to *g,* forcing coverage by No. 1. As No. 1 commits himself, our high-post man rolls to the basket, and our Weak Side Forward breaks to the foul line.

We achieve continuity in this attack by moving the Weak Side Forward into the high post, where he can receive an outlet pass should the deep guard and Pivot Man fail to score. In that case, *P* swings across to the opposite side of the foul lane, still deep, and *F* is in good position either to take a jump shot or to hit in to *g* or *P,* who are now at the base ends of our offensive triangle. (See *Diagram 76.*)

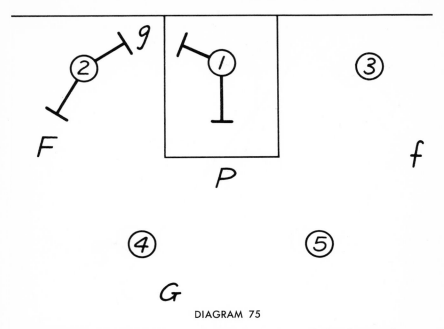

DIAGRAM 75

Attacking the 2-3 Zone. No. 1 and No. 2 must cover three offensive players once g has moved deep inside the zone.

Our 1-3-1 attack against this particular zone is also effective when
the Pivot Man at the high-post position gets the original pass from G.
The Pivot Man's own pass options are shown in *Diagram 77*. In this
situation both of our forwards move in quickly to good jump-shot positions, and our deep guard is still in good position for a shot, if the opportunity presents itself for a quick pass in to him.

Whenever the high-post man gets the ball, the middle zone man,
No. 1, must cover him, which opens up the baseline for a pass. If the
No. 2 and No. 3 men collapse, our forwards are open for short jump
shots.

The only weakness in this attack is in the fact that we have a guard
inside, which seemingly leaves us vulnerable to a fast break. Offensively,
however, we are rebounding with "three-and-a-half men," and we score
frequently on rebound shots. We play the long rebound, have one man
back on safety, and try to prevent the pitch-out by tying up the defensive
rebounder.

During the 1961-62 season we were fortunate enough to have as
regular guards two players perfectly suited to this attack. Tom Thacker,

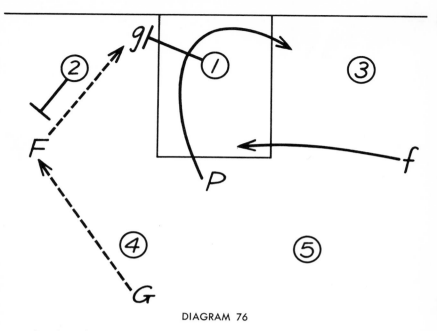

DIAGRAM 76

Attacking the 2-3 Zone. G passes to F, forcing No. 2 to cover F. F passes to g forcing No. 1 to cover g. P rolls to basket, and f breaks to the foul line. g either shoots against the one-on-one or passes to P. g can also pass out to f.

a converted forward, went in and took the deep position where his re-bounding abilities assisted our big men in stopping any intended fast break right at the source. And back in the safety position we had Tony Yates, our great defensive guard, as insurance. As a result, we were seldom bothered by a fast break out of this particular zone.

We attack the 2-1-2 Zone in exactly the same way we attack the 2-3 Zone, by sending a guard inside and executing our options as I have just described.

Attack Against the 1-3-1 Zone. Against the 1-3-1 Zone our guards maintain their normal positions, which follows our rule for odds-and-evens. Our forwards take positions on the baseline, one on the right and one on the left, each 10 to 15 feet from the basket. Our Pivot Man assumes the high-post position. (See *Diagram 78.*)

The 2-1-2 offensive alignment that we have established in *Diagram 78* should force the defense to drop back into a 2-3 Zone. If it does, we will hit our Pivot Man at his high-post position. This is especially effective

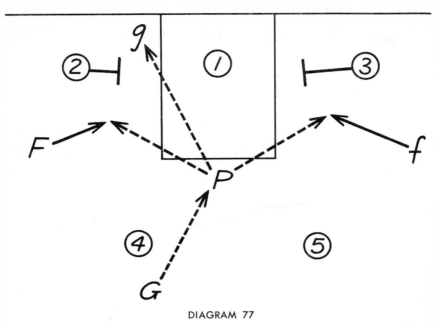

DIAGRAM 77

Attacking the 2-3 Zone. Pass options of the high-post man against this defense. Note that g has gone deep.

if the opposition plays its own pivot man as the deep man in the zone, since our Pivot Man can then take advantage of the overmatched one-on-one situation, either to get off a shot or to feed a guard or forward for a 10 to 15 foot jump shot. If the defense is strong enough to keep the Pivot Man from feeding the forwards in their deep positions, we will not be able to force the 2-3 alignment, and we must use another approach to this zone.

In *Diagram 79* I have illustrated how we set up an overload, with our best corner shooter taking the corner shot. Our deep man closest to the foul lane acts as a decoy to open up the shot as much as possible, place himself in rebound position, or place himself in a corner position in case we have to bring the ball all the way around the horn for a shot from the opposite side.

Although standard zones usually inhibit the offense as far as screening is concerned, we are often successful in screening for a baseline shot when operating against a 1-3-1 Zone. This attack, shown in *Diagram 80,* is a continuity offense off the overload and corner shot described in *Diagram 79.* If you study *Diagram 79,* you will note that f and P can

143

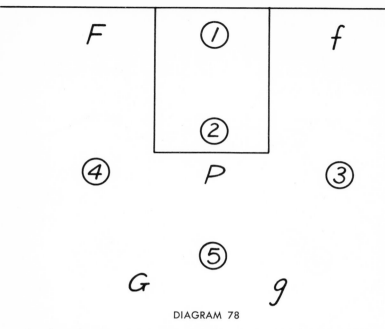

DIAGRAM 78

Attacking the 1-3-1 Zone. Sending forwards deep should force defense into a 2-3 Zone. If so, then P can be fed from outside.

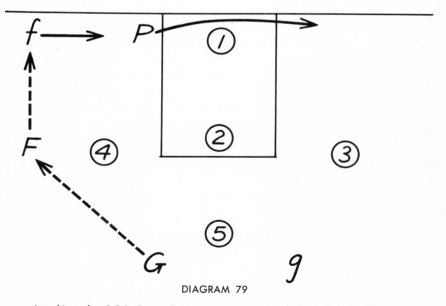

DIAGRAM 79

Attacking the 1-3-1 Zone. Setting up an overload. Best corner shooter should be f. P breaks across foul lane as decoy and possible rebounder. If shot cannot be taken, f passes out to F again and moves toward basket.

move into deep positions, on either side of the foul lane, as indicated. Assuming that the corner shot could not be taken, and that the ball has been brought back outside, now study *Diagram 80*. Here you will see that P swings back under the basket for the shot, while f screens out the deep middle defensive man.

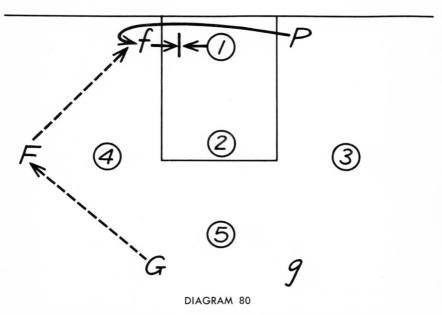

DIAGRAM 80

A Baseline Screen. P doubles back across the foul lane and screens for f who has moved close and taken a pass from F.

As a standard practice, I would suggest that any zone in which two men are tandem in the foul lane (in line one behind the other) be attacked by setting up an offensive triangle with a high post and two deep men. Feed the high post, and let him feed the deep men as they screen for each other.

Attacks Against the 3-2 and 1-2-2 Zones. Cincinnati, because of its offensive strength inside, does not encounter the 3-2 Zone, which is weak against inside attacks. If we had to face such a defense, however, I would put my best turn-around shooter and passer in the high-post position, send two tall men deep along the foul lane, keep my guards in normal outside positions, and feed the high-post man. This would force the deep defensive men into tandem positions, and allow the high-post man to hit the forwards as they screened for each other. If the defense did not go into tandem positions in the foul lane, my high-post man could shoot all night. In *Diagram 81* I have shown our positions against this type of zone, and in *Diagram 82* I have shown the screening possibilities, if the tandem positions are taken. Notice that guard G can also hit the forwards directly.

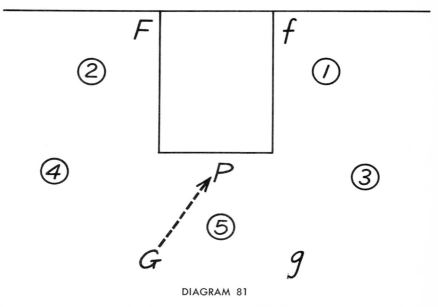

DIAGRAM 81

Attack positions against a 3-2 Zone.

Occasionally we will send our guard through the zone and pull our forwards out wide to the extended foul line in the same 1-3-1 offensive attack that we use against the 2-3 Zone described previously. This will force the players in the zone into man-to-man defensive alignments, from which we will work for a deep one-on-one shot. This is especially effective with mismatched alignments. (See *Diagram 83.*)

Diagram 83 should also reveal the tremendous weakness of a zone that is heavy outside, if its players are not skilled in man-to-man defense.

Since the 1-2-2 is merely a special case of the 3-2 Zone, we would attack it in the same way, forcing the back men into tandem positions. On occasion we would send our guard deep, as before, pulling one of the two deep zone men outside, so that our high-post man could roll to the basket behind him. Unfortunately, no one yet has given us an opportunity to try these attacks in a game.

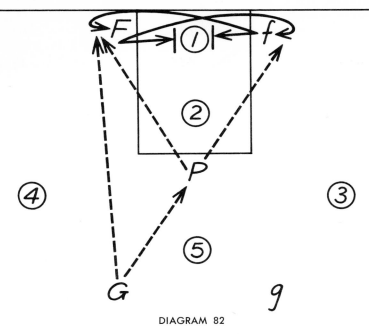

DIAGRAM 82

Options against a 3-2 Zone. Baseline screening is indicated.

Combination Defenses

I have been impressed by the spreading use of defenses that combine the man-to-man and zone principles. I am not referring to the standard box and chaser, which has four men in a 2-2 Zone, with the fifth man chasing the ball, but to a type of defense that zones the three back men and plays the two front men man-to-man. Many teams are now making effective use of such defenses because, in essence, they disrupt both a man-to-man offense and a zone offense.

In attacking these combination defenses we have tried to force them into tandem positions by setting up our offensive triangle. Our real difficulty with them, however, has arisen from a failure to recognize them. It is confusing to bring the ball up and not know if you are facing a man-to-man or a zone situation. At present, I would say that there is a definite advantage in being able to determine when a team changes from its regular defense to a combination defense. Some teams make this change after every foul shot. Some use a signal. No one we have faced used a combination defense throughout a ball game.

The adoption of combination defenses may indicate that the popu-

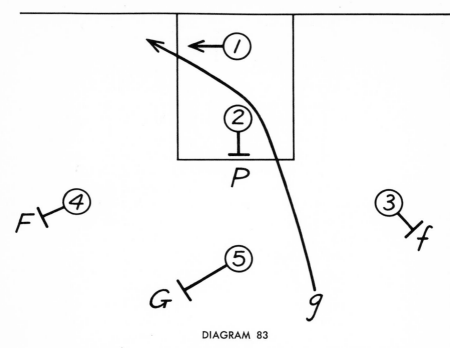

DIAGRAM 83

Attacking a zone with tandem defense in the foul lane by forcing defensive
players into man-to-man.

larity of the fast break is ebbing somewhat. When a team is willing to
let its guards go to the back line of its zone instead of waiting outside
for the outlet pass, defense is on the ascent. Although combination defenses seem bound to promise trouble to many standard offenses in use
today, the fact that they are helping to return basketball to the team is
encouraging. As team defense improves, new team offenses will have
to be improved. This is the kind of improvement that will keep basketball
alive, and I welcome it.

The fast break is the home-run of basketball. Some teams build their offense around it, and other teams go for it when the opportunity arises. Every team profits by it at one time or another. Like a home-run, the fast break is a quick, comparatively easy way to score, *if you can get it off the ground*. The ease and speed with which a fast break leads to a basket can be misleading. A number of factors must be present in a game situation before the circumstances are right for breaking down the floor offensively. Since we play a percentage game at Cincinnati, we have weighed those factors carefully, and we have rejected the fast break as our primary offensive attack. When the opportunity—in the shape of a fast defensive rebound, a quick pitchout to the side, and men in position to race downcourt—presents itself, we will not hesitate to fast break. The number of such opportunities in any particular ball game will vary, depending on the speed of the opposition, their strength on the boards, and the pattern of their offense. Our first aim on a defensive rebound is to gain possession of the ball, and, as I have pointed out earlier, recent changes in offensive rebounding tactics have made defensive rebounding more difficult than ever. Modern defenses have also made a fast break after a missed foul shot less successful than in the past, because the position of the defensive players on the foul lane now gives the team shooting the foul a much lower percentage of rebounds

14

THE FAST BREAK

than ever before. Consequently, the team shooting the foul has its back men prepared to defense a break as the foul shot is attempted.

The highest percentage of success on a fast break comes about on a sudden turnover, such as a stolen ball or an intercepted pass. Conversion from offense to defense in these situations is extremely difficult, and the chance of being caught at a two-on-one or three-on-two disadvantage is decidedly present. Using our man-to-man pressure defense, we get our share of such opportunities, but, again, they are not numerous enough for us to consider the fast break our major offensive system.

The Straight Line Fast Break

Our emphasis on simplicity of offense led us to adopt the Straight Line Fast Break as the best for our purposes. Viewing the basketball court lengthwise, we divide it into left, right, and middle lanes. Our object is to fill each lane as quickly as possible, usually with the two guards and the forward opposite the rebound. These positions are not stereotyped, however. We are more interested in having the lanes filled quickly than we are in who fills them. Our one exception is the rebounder, who must remain as safety man, defending the basket in the event the ball is intercepted. He also guards against the long pass after our fast break is successful. In the event we cannot score off the break on a good shot, we refuse to waste a shot and we bring the ball back outside for our regular offense. The safety man then resumes his normal offensive position downcourt. Should the fast-break rebound come off the boards long, or in an odd manner, so that the rebounder is outside, then the last man down the court becomes the safety man.

Diagram 84 illustrates an ideal Straight Line Fast Break. The rebound has been made by the Pivot Man, *P,* who immediately turns to the outside, holding the ball high to prevent a surprise slap at the ball by a fourth man coming in from the outside (one of the methods of stopping a fast break before it starts). The guard on the side where the ball is rebounded, *G,* moves quickly to the outside to a position on the extended foul line. The outlet pass from *P* to *G* must be fast, of course, since speed is essential at this point.

The guard opposite the rebound moves to a position in the center of the court, near the top of the foul circle, then cuts up the middle and receives a pass from *G,* who may have started dribbling up the side by now. The forward, *f,* who is opposite the rebound, fills in the third lane.

You will notice that *F* follows the action as trailer. He should stay

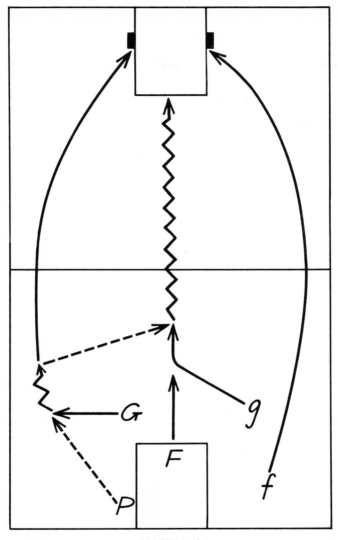

DIAGRAM 84

The Straight Line Fast Break. Side lanes and middle lane are filled. Ideal situation has middle-lane man bringing the ball down. This is the simplest way to break, after a defensive rebound. Rebound man without the ball becomes the trailer. Rebound man with the ball always becomes the safety man.

about 12 feet behind the middle-lane man, and it is his responsibility to help direct the break by calling the situation to the lane men, letting them know if they have a three-on-one, three-on-two, or three-on-three.

Unless the middle-lane man with the ball can drive all the way in for an easy lay-up, he should not go beyond the offensive foul line. The side-lane men should move as quickly as possible to positions on both sides of the foul lane near the buffer-zone area. These men have now formed the *offensive triangle,* a pattern that offers the best chance of successful completion of the fast break.

Once the middle-lane man has reached the foul line with the ball, control, not speed, becomes his primary concern. It is at this point that most errors are committed. For this reason our players are taught to regard the foul line as a barrier, *unless the middle lane to the basket is clear.* The man with the ball must be able to discipline himself in an instant, assess the defensive situation, and make the right pass. He must also be prepared to move in and rebound when the shot is made. The player who is the best ball-handler and playmaker on the team is the ideal man for the middle lane.

Finishing the Fast Break

The pitchout may be perfect, the break down the floor may go smoothly, and the three breaking men may race into their offensive positions without opposition, but none of this will matter if your offense falls apart at this point. Finishing the fast break successfully is the only thing that makes the rest of the action worthwhile. And a successful finish depends on split-second reactions to the defense in and near the foul lane. Quick passes here are essential, and quick thinking is required, if a score is to be made.

A good defensive team will manage to get one or even two men into the foul lane. If one, then the three offensive men should be able to make a basket on a series of short passes and good fakes. If two defensive men are guarding the foul lane, they will usually take tandem positions. A pass to either of the side-lane men should pull the low man on the tandem off to the ball side. If the top man stays high, the play should then be finished as illustrated in *Diagram 85.*

Should the top man drop back as the pass is made to a side-lane man, great speed will be necessary to defeat him. (This is the defense we teach our own players, to force the shot from outside, and we consider it the best way to cover the three-on-two.)

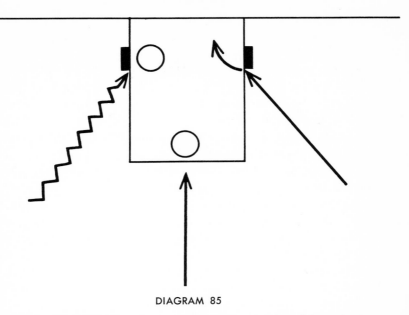

DIAGRAM 85

Finishing the Fast Break. Three-on-two against a tandem defense in the lane. Middle-lane man has passed to side-lane man who dribbles in, pulling low man on tandem out of position. Other side-lane man breaks for basket.

Since we instruct our players never to wait for the ball when the break begins, but to get down the court as rapidly as possible, the man who gets the pitchout may not be able to hit the middle-lane man. In such a case, the middle-lane man should continue without the ball, angling off to the open lane as the man with the ball cuts to the middle.

Sometimes a side-lane man will have the ball and be far in advance of the other two men breaking downcourt. As he dribbles to his spot near the buffer zone, he has two choices. If possible, he makes the shot; if he cannot shoot, he passes out to the middle-lane man at the foul line.

When two men, without the ball, go down the same lane, the front man is instructed to go to the buffer zone in the filled lane and then cut across to the opposite side to fill out the offensive triangle. Vocal help from the second man is necessary in this situation, since it is hard for the front man to recognize when it has happened.

The successful finish of any fast break depends on

1. Ball control at the foul line.
2. The offensive triangle.

3. A minimum of quick passes.
4. Vocal instructions by the men involved.

Needless to say, the ability of the players and the speed of their reactions to the defense determine the final outcome.

The Offensive Trailer

In the previous paragraphs I have assumed that the breaking team has established a three-on-one or a three-on-two advantage. Let us now assume that they face a three-on-three as the fast break nears its finish. Success is now in the hands of the trailer.

Moving downcourt behind the play, the trailer is in position to direct operations. If he sees the possibility of a drive down the middle, we want him to shout, "Trailer!" On this command, the middle-lane man dribbles to the side, and the trailer drives straight ahead, looking for a pass. If this maneuver is successful, the trailer either drives all the way for a shot, or he becomes the point on a three-on-two triangle now established ahead of the middle-lane man and the middle-lane-man's guard.

The trailer may also set up a play, even though he has no opportunity to drive down the middle. Seeing the three-on-three develop in front of him, and having no chance to lend a hand, he calls, "Three-on-three!" in our system. This signal informs the middle-lane man that he is to pass to one of the side-lane men as they approach the foul line and foul line extended. Immediately after passing (see *Diagram 86*), the middle-lane man cuts opposite the ball to pick the defensive man on that side. If this pick *forces a switch,* the middle-lane man rolls to the basket, takes a return pass and lays it up.

If no switch is made on the play shown in *Diagram 86,* the man with the ball either fights the one-on-one or takes advantage of any defensive lapse that occurs. Worked correctly, this fast break finish is an excellent example of split-second timing.

Summary

This particular Straight Line Fast Break has served us well through two successive championship seasons. As our only run-and-shoot offense, it can be incorporated into one drill (see chapter 10) and perfected quickly and efficiently. Added to our general pattern offense, it enables us to hit fast when circumstances make running desirable. Although we are not a fast-breaking team, we have profited by the element of sur-

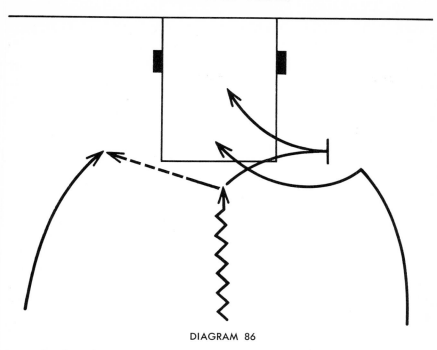

DIAGRAM 86

Finishing the Fast Break. Three-on-three at the foul line. Middle-lane man passes off to side-lane man and then cuts right to pick. If switch is made, middle-lane man rolls off pick to the basket.

prise this simple sweep contributes to our attack. By keeping it simple, we have tried to eliminate the haphazard, too-hasty play that often characterizes run-shoot-run basketball.

As proponents of deliberate, disciplined, power basketball, the Cincinnati Bearcats do not allow any team to force them into a running game. Instead, we attempt to make every opponent play our game, at our tempo, by applying the one formula that sums up the entire offensive-defensive basketball system I have presented in this book. That formula goes like this:

$$POISE + PRIDE + PRESSURE = SUCCESS$$

No coach should be satisfied with less.

What is so special about Cincinnati basketball that a book needed to be written about it?

This is a fair question. To some readers, who consider won-lost records a measure of success, the answer is evident. To others it may not be that simple. Every day I get letters from coaches and players and basketball fans, asking for information about giving the game back to the team. Perhaps those who are close to the game are growing weary of the annual search for bigger and better super-stars. As basketball threatens to become the province of the superman and the publicity man, the demand for greater and greater individual performance and wilder and wilder press notices seems ready to eliminate the team and the coach altogether. I like to think that the Cincinnati story can help change the direction in which the game is headed.

Basketball should be a test of teams. And teams should be composed of players who are trained in "total basketball," offense *and* defense, shooting *and* guarding—we should not be satisfied with less. The star system, domination by the "big man," pressure for more and more scoring, a helter-skelter, run-shoot-run exhibition—none of these can substitute for the test of team offense against team defense, coaching strategy against coaching strat-

15

RANDOM

OBSERVATIONS

ON A GREAT SPORT

egy, and application of basketball fundamentals to the game.

For a good many years a good many coaches have been saying, "There is a place for the little man in basketball," and, "Let's put defense back in the game." Any criticism of the star system was interpreted as "sour grapes," however, and the plea for opportunities for the smaller player and more defense were considered the alibis of losers. I like to think the Cincinnati story can help change that, too.

Cincinnati has not been alone in its effort to teach "total basketball." Twice in recent years a tight defense and a disciplined pattern offense took the University of California to the NCAA Finals. In our own tough Missouri Valley Conference more and more teams are playing "total basketball" and getting tougher and tougher. As I tour the country during a basketball season I see indications that a basketball era is coming to a close, and that a new and greater era is destined to take its place. Spectators are learning to appreciate the drama and excitement of team basketball. Their enjoyment of the game is increasing.

These changes do not imply that the player with outstanding talent is now doomed to ride the bench. Far from it. In becoming all-around basketball players, these fortunate few will discover that the game is more stimulating, more challenging, and far more rewarding than ever before.

I do not mean to take anything away from the performances and records of the players who have emblazoned their names on the pages of basketball history in the past. An Oscar Robertson comes along once in a lifetime, and his exceptional talents add excitement and glory to the game. But a basketball system cannot be built on the assumption that every year will bring another Robertson, and another after that, and then another, forever. Nor is it sufficient to create a super-star in the press when you lack one on the floor.

Too often the lessons that could be learned from the performance of a truly great basketball player are overlooked. Too much attention to final records ignores the means by which these records were achieved. Boys who should be playing basketball are scared off because of the mistaken notion that basketball stars are born that way, or spring fully equipped from some celestial locker room. Too little is written or told of the years of grueling practice, of the tremendous will to succeed, or of the diligent concentration on fundamentals that lead to excellence.

As an assistant coach at the University of Cincinnati I worked with Jack Twyman, the great pro sharpshooter, and Oscar Robertson during their undergraduate days. Neither man ever slighted a practice session.

Neither was content to rest on his press clippings, or felt that his performance could not be improved. Both were team men. Robertson's record for assists is well known. Twyman's responsibility for his teammates goes far beyond the basketball floor. His work with and for Maurice Stokes, the player struck down by illness at the height of his career, is a lesson in living. Much of what I saw and knew of Twyman and Robertson during their college careers, their work on fundamentals, their hundred per cent effort in every practice session, and their desire to excel, should be listed with their records for the benefit of young players.

I asked Robertson recently what advice he would give to a boy who was interested in playing basketball, and he said, "There is only one word—fundamentals."

Oscar began playing basketball on the sandlots before he attended high school. "You learned the one-on-one there," he says. "And if you really wanted to play, you worked on your jump shots and corner shots and foul shots. At first I used to hold the ball back on my palm—then I read a book by Claire Bee. He said hold it up on the fingertips, so I worked on that. I still work on it. All the fundamentals. In high school my coach, Ray Crowe, made me work harder. He showed me I didn't know it all, helped me see I could always learn something from somebody. Every practice, high school or college or the pro's, I always tried to do better."

There is no easy path to the top.

Jack Twyman, whose collegiate and professional records identify him as one of the truly great shooters of modern basketball, did not make his high school team until his senior year. "I went out for it three times and didn't make it," he told me. "So I made up my mind I would have to work harder. I decided that if I worked an hour longer than everybody else in practice I would improve faster than they did. Practice is the only way to learn."

Twyman, a shooting perfectionist, developed his own practice routine. He still follows it. "I shoot 200 jump shots first. Then about 150 set shots. After that 100 to 150 foul shots. Not just playing around, you understand. I keep track of every shot—two out of three, five out of seven—every one is important. I try to pressure myself. If you're going to throw it up at the basket and not care, you might as well not practice."

The same story runs through the records of every champion, the same striving for improvement through practice. The championship team is no different. If the team can be convinced that the old-fashioned virtues of hard work, pride, and desire can lead to success, then half the battle is won.

All coaches are asked at one time or another to list the attributes they look for in a boy. I would put "attitude" at the head of the list. After that I am interested in an active ball player who can jump, a good ball-handler who has touch, and a boy with strength enough to mix under the boards. Proper attitude, however, is the one essential that makes all the others usable in our system. Our players must be willing to learn, willing to work, willing to sacrifice, and willing to become "red shirts" when the occasion demands it. Our roster contains the names of players who gave full effort to the team, some for three varsity years, without public recognition. All teams have similar rosters. Ron Reis, our reserve center, spent three years in the shadow of Paul Hogue, yet never "dogged it" in practice. Jim Calhoun, a fine shooting guard, helped us by coming off the bench whenever we needed him, but more important, he gave the starting five all it could handle in scrimmages, year after year.

In the summer of 1961 the Cincinnati team was privileged to visit the Philippines on a goodwill tour sanctioned by the State Department. It was an inspiration for all of us, players and coaches alike, to see the impact that basketball has made on other countries of the world. In Manila's 30,000-seat Araneta Coliseum we played eight of the finest amateur teams in the islands, and we were impressed by the speed, agility, and shooting skill of our opponents. Those who say that the little man has no place in basketball should have been there. Basketball has become the national pastime in the Philippines, and 28,000 spectators turned out for our final game against their 1960 Olympic team. Height and defense made the difference in that game, but I predict the Philippines will surprise a lot of people in 1964. In every clinic that we held out there, our listeners were *eager* listeners, anxious to learn. It is the same in other parts of the world, wherever basketball has been started, and wherever American teams have visited. Basketball is becoming international, and we will have to continue to improve, if we hope to continue our success in the sport we invented. I would like to see that improvement take the direction of team basketball.

In order to justify its existence in the high school or college program, basketball should provide an educational experience. Lessons in sportsmanship, cooperation, and discipline can and should be taught on the court. Modern collegiate teams, traveling thousands of miles, staying in fine hotels, and appearing before millions of spectators on television, must be creditable representatives of their schools. Two of the most quoted remarks in the sports world are also two of the most unfortunate. "We don't have much chance of winning this year, so we're building character," is one, and the other is, "Nice guys finish last." Character and its byproducts *are* the concern of every coach at the high school and college level. It is our responsibility to turn out gentlemen.

Not all aspects of the game are serious, of course. I do not pretend that the future of the world and all its generations depends on basketball. Big-time collegiate basketball is first of all a game, and the player who does not enjoy it should stay out of it. It is, of course, far more enjoyable to win than it is to lose. But the world does not end with a loss on the court.

Twice I have seen Cincinnati teams facing the end of whatever hopes they have had for a successful season. In 1960-61 we lost two consecutive conference games before January 1st. In 1961-62 we lost two conference games, also early in the season. On both occasions the players knew that only a miracle could get us into the NCAA Tournament. On both occasions the miracle was performed by the players. They determined to become a team, and in both cases went undefeated for the remainder of the season.

During the years that I have been connected with basketball, as a player and coach, I have formed some definite opinions about all aspects of the game, but I do not claim to know everything there is to know. Every coach must keep an open mind and be flexible enough in his own thinking to recognize useful innovations developed by others. In turn, a coach of any stature whatsoever owes it to the game to pass on to others the ideas that have been successful for him. The greatest era in basketball is just beginning. New techniques, like the combination defense, are in their infancy. Total, team basketball is going to uncover strategies of offense and defense that have been unknown in the past. Individual skills will still be in demand, but they will be incorporated into team systems that free the individual from the pressure of having to carry a whole ball team. Continuous, fast-moving pattern offenses, striking from a variety of directions, will combine the timing and execution of the old set-play with the speed and excitement of the fast break, without reverting to either. As defensive and rebounding techniques improve, run-shoot-run basketball will decline. Scores will not be so high as in the past, but the drama of superb offense against superb defense will be a welcome change from the shooting exhibitions spectators have been watching.

ILLUSTRATION XII

The first of two consecutive NCAA championship trophies is earned by Cincinnati, using the system of "total basketball" described in this book.

RANDOM OBSERVATIONS ON A GREAT SPORT

The new era of basketball, while returning to the original spirit of the game, will not be a return to slow-down, low-score or no-score, uninspired contests. It will feature a minimum of dribbling, fast passing, and a maximum of cutting, picking and screening, with split-second timing necessary for a successful attack. Spectators will learn more of the strategy of offense and defense and will better understand the finer points of the game.

These changes will not come overnight, of course. Perhaps a new generation of basketball coaches will have to work out the final ramifications. But little by little the new era is creeping up on us. I think it will be worth seeing.

In Cincinnati the field house is sold out for another season, and the Bearcats are taking the Swing-and-Go, the Backdoor Trap, and the High Post on another round through the Missouri Valley Conference. Selling defense is easier now, and working for the close-in, high-percentage shot has become second nature to the players. The "red shirts" are making it tough for the starting five, as usual, and the thud of the ball and the cries of "Pick! Pick!" are music to a coach's ears.

Life could be worse.

INDEX

INDEX

INDEX

INDEX

INDEX

INDEX

T

U

INDEX

DATE DUE

OCT 12 '63			
OCT 29 '63			
DEC 4 '63			
FEB 25 '64			
FEB 27 '65			
NOV 5 '66			
JUL 30 '80			
3-2-93			
GAYLORD			PRINTED IN U S A